About the Author

Peter Lemesurier was for many years a senior modern languages teacher and professional translator. He is the author of the best-selling *The Great Pyramid Decoded*, *Beyond All Belief*, *The Cosmic Eye*, *Gospel of the Stars*, *The Great Pyramid: Your Personal Guide*, *The Healing of the Gods* and *This New Age Business*. Widely acknowledged as a leading authority on Nostradamus, he is the author of a number of books on the seer including *Nostradamus — The Next 50 Years*, *Nostradamus: The Final Reckoning* and the definitive English language reference book, *The Nostradamus Encyclopedia*.

The Essential Nostradamus

Piatkus Guides

Other titles in this series include

A PIATKUS GUIDE

The Essential Nostradamus

Peter Lemesurier

PIATKUS

Neither the author nor the publisher is responsible for the expressed views or predictions of Nostradamus, nor do they necessarily subscribe to them. Readers' reactions to the prophecies are entirely their own responsibility, as are the results of any application they may make of Nostradamus's prophetic techniques. While all interpretations are offered in good faith, no guarantee is implied or should be inferred regarding their accuracy.

© 1999 Peter Lemesurier

First published in 1999 by
Judy Piatkus (Publishers) Ltd
5 Windmill Street, London W1P 1HF

The author asserts his moral rights in this book under the Copyright, Designs and Patents Act of 1988

A catalogue record for this book is available from the British Library

ISBN 0-7499-1868-3

Verse extracts on pages 18, 27, 35, 40, 69, and 83 are reproduced by kind permission of the Godsfield Press

Set in 12.5/14pt Perpetua
Typeset by Action Publishing Technology Limited, Gloucester
Printed & bound in Great Britain by
Mackays of Chatham PLC

Contents

Five hundred years, then more heed they shall take
Of him who was the jewel of his age.
Suddenly then shall light resplendent break
Such as that time's approval to engage.

Nostradamus: *Les Propheties*, 1555 (III.94)

Introduction

Nostradamus is possibly the most misunderstood and misrepresented of all the world's prophets. This book is designed first to help put the record straight, then to help you to understand him and his prophecies, and finally to show you how to apply his prophetic techniques for yourself.

As a 16th-century French seer who had inherited Jewish blood from his father's ancestors and the gift of foresight allegedly from his mother's, Nostradamus saw himself as continuing a long double line of prophets. One of these (the biblical line) led all the way from Isaiah to John of Patmos. The other (the pagan line) led from the ancient Greek oracles of Branchidai and Delphi to the Sibylline oracle of Cumae and the great Roman poet Virgil (whom Nostradamus idolised).

He was thus very much a man of his time, struggling – like most other intellectuals from the Pope down – to reconcile the beliefs and dogmas of Christianity with the newly rediscovered insights and practices of ancient paganism.

Yet not too many of us are familiar with the feverish climate of those times or its innate contradictions. Consequently there are those who, even today, doubt that such a strange person could ever have existed. There are others who have seen Nostradamus as such a cloudy, almost legendary figure as to justify hanging all sorts of gratuitous myths and superstitions around his neck. Yet others, inevitably, have sought to grow rich on the back of this tendency by publishing accounts of him and his work that bear little, if any relation to the facts.

As an aid to dispelling some of the more persistent of these myths and misunderstandings – as well as to orientating yourself within this book – you will find that the text is interspersed with some of the more frequently asked questions about Nostradamus and their answers.

My own interest in Nostradamus is long-standing. As a teacher of modern languages and translator I have been able to study the original texts in detail and produced the first sequenced English translation of over 400 of Nostradamus's prophecies in 1993, *Nostradamus – the Next 50 Years*. In the course of my research I have developed a close working relationship with the staff of Nostradamus's house in Salon and with leading French experts on the seer. As a result I was able to produce in 1997 the only up-to-date, definitive English language reference book currently available, *The Nostradamus Encyclopedia*. I hope this book will awaken your own interest and help you come to a more complete understanding of Nostradamus's life and work.

1

The Budding Prophet

By the early 16th century the French Renaissance was in full swing. There was a ferment of classical ideas in the air, and scholars of all descriptions were becoming positively drunk with the literature, art and architecture not only of ancient Greece, but especially of Rome. Nobody was anybody who could not read and write Latin, and educated society was growing more and more besotted with the idea of returning to the glories of the classical past.

Yet, curiously, the idea of 'progress' was entirely absent — indeed, it would not finally arise for another three hundred years or so. Whether or not because of this, society itself remained firmly stuck in medieval mode. The France over which King Louis XII reigned — threatened as it was by Spain and the Holy Roman Empire to the east and west, and by the ever-expanding Muslim Ottoman empire to the south and south-east — was a chaotic, patchwork kingdom of differing laws, customs and forms of local government. There were no roads or public transport worth mentioning, let alone any public postal service. As the 'Little Ice Age' of later in the century started to make itself felt, widespread penury, star-vation, unemployment, inflation, war, squalor and pestilence were never far away, while the bloodiest era of religious conflicts and massacres that Europe has ever known was only just around the corner.

It was into this strangely contradictory mixture of circum-stances, that Michel de Nostredame was born at St-Rémy-de-Provence on 14 December 1503, and duly baptised into the Christian faith. He was apparently the eldest of at least nine children known to have been born to a prosperous local merchant named Jaume (i.e. James) de Nostredame and his wife Reynière de St-Rémy.

Jaume's father, the Avignon merchant Guy Gassonet, may have come of ancient Jewish-Spanish stock. He had converted from Judaism to Roman Catholicism in around 1463 and taken the name Pierre de Nostredame (Peter of Our Lady) appar-ently after the name of the presiding bishop and the feast-day on which the ceremony took place (presumably 2 July, Feast of the Visitation of the Blessed Virgin Mary). Repudiating his second, Jewish wife, who refused to convert, he had then married Blanche, a Christian who obviously had a mind of her own and so preferred to call herself Blanche *de Sainte-Marie*.

So it was that both their son Jaume and *his* son Michel inherited the name 'de Nostredame', which the latter would eventually Latinise into 'Nostradamus' after the scholastic fashion of the day.

To start with, the young seer-to-be seems to have been educated by his maternal great-grandfather Jean de St-Rémy, a local physician and sometime Town Treasurer. It may be assumed that the boy was instructed in Greek, Latin, mathematics and the then-still-undifferentiated mysteries of astronomy and astrology, as well as being given a smattering of chemistry, medicine and herbalism.

Q. Isn't it true that both Nostradamus's grandfathers were royal physicians at the court of Good King René of Provence?

A. No. This is unfortunately no more than wishful thinking, originally put about by his eldest son César, who was always keen to gild the lily where his family was concerned. As we noted above, Michel's paternal grandfather Pierre de Nostredame was simply a merchant at Avignon. His maternal grandfather René de St-Rémy seems to have been equally undistinguished, and died before the child was born. As for René's father Jean (Nostradamus's maternal *great-*grandfather), he was admittedly a doctor, but his royal connections are likely to have been limited to treating the King during periodic royal visits to St-Rémy.

The celestial studies particularly seem to have struck home, as did a passionate interest in the well-preserved classical relics of the area – notably the gate and mausoleum of the ancient Graeco-Roman city of Glanum, just up the hill to the south of the town beside the priory of St-Paul-de-Mausole. There was also the nearby Roman stone-quarry whose long-abandoned galleries and caves were now used mainly by goat-herds and their flocks, and whose centre was marked by an extraordinary pinnacle of rock that is still known locally as *la Pyramide* (presumably a corruption of *la pierre en mi* – 'the rock in the middle').

It is no surprise, then, that all of these were subsequently to be mentioned in his prophecies.

At the age of 16 the growing youth – already noted, it seems, for his passionate interest in astrology and his facetious sense of humour – went on to complete his education at Avignon, where he possibly gained his baccalaureate degree before the university was disbanded in 1520 in the face of a mounting plague epidemic that was sweeping through Provence at the time.

He then became a wandering apothecary before returning to the celebrated Montpellier Medical Faculty in 1529 to take his doctorate. True, he was kicked out of the student body again a fortnight before his course even began, on the grounds that he had not only been a despised apothecary, but as such had been rude about doctors into the bargain. There is not even any record of his re-admission. But the fact that he would frequently refer in his later writings to other Montpellier *alumni* of the time suggests that he somehow managed to get himself reinstated and in due course gained his doctorate.

Q. Don't numerous books state that he in fact went to Montpellier much earlier, in 1522, took his baccalaureate there in 1525, and after his doctorate went on to teach in the Medical Faculty?

A. There is absolutely no record of any of this, and he himself states perfectly clearly that he spent the years from 1520 to 1529 wandering the countryside in search of cures and natural medicines. Moreover, by 1531 he seems to have been on the move again – which effectively rules out the last-mentioned possibility altogether.

Nostredame now went on to practise medicine for some 16 years, first at Agen in the south-west, then at various other towns and cities, and seems to have shown particular interest in treating the plague. His main training in this took place at

Marseille in 1544, under the celebrated physician Louis Serre. He then went on to take personal control of other outbreaks at Aix-en-Provence, Salon and possibly Lyon. His best-selling cookbook (actually entitled the *Traité des fardemens et confitures*, or 'Treatise on Cosmetics and Conserves') describes the outbreak at Aix in the most graphic and gruesome detail.

Despite the resulting public acclaim, however, he confesses that none of his remedies worked – not even the famous rose-pills for which he actually supplies the recipe in the *Traité*, and which he seems to have used at least as much to protect himself as to treat his patients. The fact that town after town employed him as official Plague Supremo suggests that he was valued not as a mere pill-pusher but because he initiated some kind of civic health programme, possibly based on the writings of the ancient Greek 'Father of Medicine', Hippocrates.

Q. I have read that his plague treatment involved the use of large quantities of running water, and that he absolutely refused to bleed his patients as tradition required. Is this true?

A. Yes and no. While there is no direct evidence that running water played much part in his cures, he did later show a keen interest in it, even helping to finance a major irrigation scheme in the area of Salon. This might suggest that he applied the healthy environmental precepts of Hippocrates rather more literally than many of his contemporaries. But his alleged refusal to bleed his patients is, alas, just another unsubstantiated myth. He himself states in the *Traité* that blood-letting *was* among the methods tried, albeit without success.

Recent archival research at Agen has revealed that Nostredame's first wife had been named Henriette d'Encausse. However, both she and their two children had died of some unspecified illness (probably the plague) in about 1534. In 1547, however, the now successful doctor married for a second time. Anne Ponsarde, known as 'Gemelle' (i.e. 'Twinny'), was the young widow of a rich lawyer of Salon-de-Provence called Jean Beaulme. After marrying the future seer there that year, she was to bear him six children and survive him by 16 years, finally dying in 1582.

Thus it was that Nostredame now settled down in the town with his young new wife and turned instead to the writing of annual *Almanachs* and the composition of a vast collection of prophecies intended to foretell the entire future history of the world, mainly on the basis of astrology. This was not as strange an activity for an ex-doctor as it may sound: astrology was, after all, a major part of the diagnostic armoury of physicians at the time. Besides, from about 1540 a whole panoply of astrological tables had been published, allowing anybody who was interested to work out the positions of the planets for centuries to come.

Having come to the predictive aspect of astrology rather late, however, the would-be prophet proved relatively clumsy and incompetent when it came to interpreting the minutiae of other astrologers' tables (it now appears that he never composed his own from scratch). He had only the vaguest notion of how to perform the astrologer's primary task, namely calculating the Ascendant, and was sometimes even prone to put planets in the wrong signs entirely. When challenged to draw up important clients' horoscopes he admitted privately to feeling very uncomfortable, especially if they themselves knew something about the subject, and consequently he was (on other people's evidence) prone to let the planetary ephemeris (i.e. astronomical tables) fall open at any old page, while mumbling vaguely about 'divine inspiration'.

As a result he was heavily criticised by the professional astrologers, against whom he would feel the need to defend himself in every one of his *Almanachs*. However, he himself was convinced of his prophetic abilities and soon became famous throughout France as a sage and seer. It was from about this time, consequently, that he started to Latinise his name to Nostradamus – as was the fashion of the day for anybody who fancied himself as an academic authority.

Q. Are you saying that he was no good as a prophet?

A. No, merely that he was not up to the relatively complex demands of drawing up the personal or daily horoscopes in which the more conventional astrologers specialised. The larger-scale horoscopy underlying his main prophecies, by contrast, was a much more straightforward affair, and he seems to have had little difficulty with that. Besides, he had other, more occult strings to his prophetic bow.

Nostradamus launched his first prophetic venture, the annual *Almanachs*, in 1550. These were designed largely to predict the weather and crop prospects for the coming year, mainly on the basis of astrological calculations. Military and political developments, along with important births, marriages and deaths, were also included, but only in the most veiled and generalised of terms. While he seems to have missed the *Almanach* for 1556 because, as we shall see, he was otherwise engaged during 1555 (though he himself always claimed to have written one), these continued until the very end of his life. From 1555 they also started to include summary verses of the type that were later to become famous through his major *Propheties*. And they sold like hot cakes.

At a time that was, after all, so critical from the meteorological, political, religious and military points of view, such knowledge of the future could – if reliable – be vital to people's survival. No wonder, then, that numerous forgeries too were soon appearing under Nostradamus's name.

Q. How accurate did the *Almanachs* turn out to be in practice?

A. Not particularly, if their summary *Présages* are to be believed. On such subjects as happy and unhappy events generally, wars and peace pacts or unspecified marriages and deaths among the aristocracy ('the Great', as Nostradamus continually called them), they achieved a fair measure of 'hits'. But then so many of all of these were going on at the time that almost anybody of similar intelligence might have achieved similar results. Forecasts of cold weather in the winter, likewise, scarcely took a prophet to predict, while forecasts of cold, wet summer weather became, on past evidence, increasingly safe as the century wore on and Europe's Little Ice Age tightened its grip. But Nostradamus's constant warnings of imminent Muslim invasion in the earlier *Almanachs* turned out to be a complete damp squib, at least where France was concerned.

No wonder his former fellow student, the writer François Rabelais, parodied such almanacs unmercifully!

But then what does the average reader do when this year's almanac turns out to be wrong? He or she still buys *next* year's, just in case...

Each year's *Almanach* was longer and more detailed than the one before it, until in his next-to-last one (for 1566) Nostradamus actually went through the whole year three times over — first only in the briefest of terms, giving merely a calendar, the saints' days, the phases and positions of the moon and one or two terse prophecies; then more fully, with two cryptic French or Latin prophecies for each day; and finally with a lengthy prose description of each month in turn.

For 1 July of that year — listed in the *Almanach* as the Octave of the Feast of St Joan — for example, he predicted that the full moon would occur in Capricorn at three o'clock in the morning, and mentioned *aer turbidus* ('turbid air'). In the final, prose section he mentioned all kinds of unspecified major events for the month in general involving equally unspecified kingdoms and people in authority, as well as bloody religious disputes at home and Muslim feuds abroad between sects wearing sky-blue turbans and white turbans respectively. And in the detailed central section he not only specified that the full moon of the first of the month would be in seven degrees of Capricorn and the air sticky, but offered the cryptic prediction *Estrange transmigration*.

Which is odd, given that one meaning of 'transmigration' is the wandering of the soul at death into another body ... and that it would be during the following night that Nostradamus himself would eventually die.

True, there was no other sign in this particular *Almanach* of any suspicion on the seer's part that the prediction might apply *to him*. Everything else carried on much as before.

Nevertheless, in the *Almanach* for the following year, which he had already finished before finally succumbing to dropsy, gout and general physical collapse, he did include, ostensibly for November, a verse *Présage* that reads in translation:

> *Once back from embassy, once garnered in*
> *The kingly gift, all's done: his spirit sped,*
> *The dearest of his friends, his closest kin*
> *Beside the bed and bench shall find him dead.*

It didn't say who. It didn't say where or when. Yet the fact remains that the circumstances of this predicted death turned out to be remarkably reminiscent of the seer's own, even if more appropriate to the date when it was written (the earlier part of 1556) than to the date to which it was attached in the *Almanach* for 1567.

This is absolutely typical of Nostradamus. We have a prediction that, while in this case ostensibly attached to a known date, could actually apply to anybody, anywhere, at any time. We have circumstances that, in retrospect, would seem to fulfil the prophecy in the most dramatic way.

And on such imponderables rests the renown of the man who is generally thought to be the greatest prophet since biblical times.

Was he, then, a fraud? Was he truly psychic and clairvoyant? Did he indeed have the knack of pinning down future events via astrology? Or did he merely have the equally important knack of expressing himself in such vague terms that he could never be proved wrong, and even stood a good chance of being perceived as having hit the jackpot?

The answers are probably 'Yes, yes, yes and yes.'

Nostradamus, in other words, was indeed a prophet, and (as we shall go on to discover) the master of an extraordinary astrological technique for predicting the future. Yet at the same time he was enough of a charlatan (as, curiously enough, great spiritual and esoteric figures often are) to be a master of mystification, mumbo jumbo and sheer personal propaganda as well.

This may be a sobering thought to those who have hitherto considered him some kind of superhuman magician or even semi-divine seer – and a distinctly worrying one for the less reputable parts of the flourishing Nostradamus industry.

But at least, by showing us that he was a human being like anyone else, it holds out some hope for us mere mortals of being able to follow in his illustrious footsteps. And certainly it helps prepare us for what was to follow.

2

The Seer of Salon

It was in May 1555 — the same year as the appearance of the first verse *Présages* in the *Almanachs*, and the year after some notable local 'omens' in the form of a falling meteorite and the births of a two-headed child at Sénas and a two-headed kid at Aurons — that the first instalment of Nostradamus's *Propheties* for the entire future history of the world eventually appeared in print.

Q. I thought it was supposed to be a two-headed *foal*?

A. Unfortunately some popular commentators can't tell the difference between French *chevreau* (kid) and *cheval* (horse). This is just one minor example of the many schoolboy howlers that tend to litter English-language books on Nostradamus.

Published by Macé Bonhomme of Lyon, the book contained just 353 prophecies in verse out of a planned thousand. The reason for the odd number seems to have been a purely practical one. Publishers tended (and still tend) to work in multiples of 16 pages, and if Nostradamus had submitted 400 verses, say, the 92 pages that the text took up would have been the next practical number below what would actually have been required. There were, after all, further instalments to follow, and it would be for the retailer or purchaser eventually to bind them all together ...

Q. I thought his book was called the *Centuries*?

A. No. No edition of the *Propheties* actually bears this title. Nostradamus merely refers to each of the ten books of verses that were eventually to appear as a '*century*' – i.e. a collection, or book, of a hundred. This was a perfectly normal way to describe them at the time. For this reason the word *Centuries* is commonly used today to distinguish the original prophecies from the additional *Présages* and *Sixains* that were included in later editions.

The verses – all designed (though not always too successfully) as decasyllabic four-liners, or quatrains – were beautifully printed and decorated. However, they were not in any kind of sensible order. Evidently the seer had simply written them down as they came to him, then numbered the result in sequence within each *Century*. Consequently there was no obvious way of telling which prophecy went with which, or even what order they should be read in. In most cases there was no obvious way, either, of telling just *when* each prophecy was intended for.

All this is distinctly worrying, given that if your dentist doesn't say *when* he or she is going to fix your teeth, there is effectively no appointment ...

To make matters worse, the language was also decidedly

obscure — far more so than in the *Présages* — and the poetic technique rudimentary, if not downright crude. The text was stuffed with words borrowed from Greek and especially Latin, then Gallicised into pseudo-French. Even those words that could be understood sometimes seemed, like the verses themselves, to be in no sort of sensible order, and a few of them were obviously anagrammatised into the bargain, and sometimes spelt with capitals apparently in order to signal the fact. The spelling was chaotic, the punctuation very basic and the crude, infinitive form of the verb freely used as a kind of future tense — with *regner* being substituted for *regnera*, for example.

What, then, was the prophet up to?

Various theories have been put forward. Here are some of them:

1. He was illiterate.
2. The prophecies are just meaningless gobbledygook and not to be taken seriously.
3. He didn't really intend his verses to be understood at all, but preferred that future interpreters should let their imagination roam freely on the basis of what he had written.
4. He was really thinking in Latin — or even *writing* in Latin, then translating the results into French.
5. He intended the whole thing to be treated as a set of anagrams for anybody to make of them what they could.
6. He was writing in some other sort of code.
7. The various prophecies are intended to be identified and understood only after the event.

Unfortunately, there is absolutely no evidence for any of these theories. It is quite clear from his other writings that he was far from illiterate — on the contrary, like many of his educated contemporaries, he was possibly too literate for his own good. His spelling was chaotic simply because the very idea of 'correct spelling' did not exist at the time.

Q. Isn't it possible to work out what Nostradamus means simply by looking up each word in an ordinary French–English dictionary?

A. Emphatically not. For a start, you won't find most of them in it — at least not as spelt. And 16th-century French words do not mean the same as 20th-century English words, any more than words in one language ever mean the same as words in another (if you doubt it, ask any French person who has never learnt a word of English!). And thirdly, language consists not merely of words, but of grammar and syntax, too — i.e. the particular, often highly sophisticated ways in which the words are modified and arranged to indicate meaning. In neither case does Nostradamus follow modern French practice, let alone the modern English equivalent.

True, the idea that Nostradamus designed his verses to be used as a kind of oracle — along, no doubt, with tea-leaves and Tarot cards — is an appealing one, especially to those too lazy to learn his language, but had he done so there would have been little point in incorporating all the historical, geographical, linguistic and astrological scholarship with which they are so obviously filled. And while the verses do show considerable Latin influence — notably that of the celebrated Roman poet and prophet Virgil — there is no indication that most of them were ever written in anything other than the French of the day. Indeed, well into the next century (as the 17th-century commentator Garencières reports) the *Propheties* were actually being used as a basic reader in French schoolrooms!

Behind the idea that the whole thing is designed to be treated as a set of anagrams, meanwhile, is the principle that in order to understand Nostradamus's verses you first have to *alter* them. This, clearly, is a counsel of despair, and opens the text up to all sorts of falsifications, conscious or otherwise. Imagine what would result if the same principle were applied to the Bible, or Mrs Beeton's cookbook, or the Ford Mondeo owner's handbook ... Had Nostradamus anywhere indicated that his prophecies were in anagram form, of course, there might be some justification for this approach. But in fact he nowhere does so – and neither is there any specific suggestion that he wrote in code.

As for the idea of interpreting the prophecies only after the event, this is merely a charter for reading into them anything you like – and one that many commentators duly grab with both hands.

The evidence instead suggests that for all his undoubted prophetic gift and vaulting originality the seer was a somewhat vague-minded, shambolic character who merely did his best with the tools at his disposal. He also lacked the brilliant, incisive mind – and the time – that would have enabled him to carry out such intricate and demanding tasks as anagrammatisation and/or encoding in the first place, let alone the extreme multi-linguistic contortions that some of the more credulous observers insist on ascribing to him. After all, he clearly had the greatest of difficulty merely in squaring what he had to say with writing four lines of perfectly ordinary verse ...

The fact is, of course, that mystery was always the stock-in-trade of any would-be prophet, and given that Nostradamus had to avoid treading on all kinds of sensitive toes, especially among the influential religious, he had to watch what he said. The use of deliberately obscure language filled this need admirably. Besides, the vaguer he could be, the better the chances that he might be proved right and the less the chances that he might be proved wrong.

Q. Didn't Nostradamus write as obscurely as possible in order to escape persecution by the Inquisition for black magic and witchcraft?

A. There is no evidence of this. His sole brush with the Inquisition seems to have been a summons by the Inquisition of Toulouse early in his medical career to answer questions about a facetious remark that he was alleged to have made concerning the casting of a particularly unflattering religious image. For a born humorist with clear Franciscan sympathies, there was nothing particularly outrageous about this. Whether his sudden flight from Agen at this point was connected with the Inquisition, therefore, is not known. His late first wife's family seems to have been suing him at the time, and he had also fallen out with his patron, the doctor and scholar Jules César Scaliger – who fell out with everybody. It may simply have been inner despair and mental stress that caused him to up sticks at this point and start a period of wandering all across the country.

There was admittedly, an implied suggestion of possible witchcraft during one of his later visits to Paris, though this was made not by the Inquisition but by the local justices. In any case, Nostradamus reacted once more simply by leaving in a hurry – which might add credence to the idea that his earlier departure from Agen had been similarly motivated.

However, his relations with the Church and the senior clergy seem always to have been excellent.

Then there was his decision to write in verse. This was not in fact at all unusual at the time. Besides, historically, most major prophets had done the same. Certainly it allowed him to used compressed, poetic language and vague imagery that admirably suited his purposes. Indeed, there is some evidence that he actually used the verse form – and particularly its rhyme scheme – as a source of 'inspiration', almost letting what he predicted (or at least the way he predicted it) be largely determined by the words, rather as though they were themselves in some way 'inspired'.

And, of course, verse is far easier to remember than prose, and much more difficult for would-be 'editors' to tamper with.

At which point there is Nostradamus's idol, the Roman poet Virgil, to consider. Virgil – or Maro, to use the family name by which the seer referred to him – had been regarded in his time as a prophet in his own right. Moreover, to Nostradamus's classically orientated generation he was widely regarded as the absolute prince of poets. There was every reason, therefore, for the seer to model his style on Virgil's – and notably on his perfectly normal tendency to scatter the words of each line of verse more or less at random as the rhythm demanded, while relying on Latin's helpful grammatical endings to show which word went with which. Naively, perhaps, Nostradamus seems to have taken this as *carte blanche* to do exactly the same himself, notwithstanding the fact that the French endings were not nearly as helpful.

No doubt this was one reason why the later schoolmasters were so keen to use the *Propheties* as a kind of primer.

Q. Didn't Nostradamus use lots of Latin and Greek words simply to baffle the reader?

A. Yes and no. The deliberate use of such words to enrich and ennoble the French language had been recommended by Joachim Du Bellay's seminal manifesto of 1549 entitled *La Deffence et Illustration de la Langue Françoyse*, which had the backing both of the poet Ronsard and of Nostradamus's influential admirer and academic supporter Jean Dorat. The reverberations of this idea would even influence later foreign writers such as Shakespeare, who in deference to it introduced thousands of classical words into English.

At the time when Nostradamus was writing his prophecies, then, the classicising tendency was all the rage. Consequently, it would have been surprising had he *not* crammed his verses with Latin words in particular. On the other hand, there are far more of them in the *Centuries* than in the *Présages* or the later *Sixains* — which might suggest that he could also see the prophetic advantage of pushing the idea to extremes!

No sooner was the first instalment of the *Propheties* published than he was summoned to Paris on behalf of Queen Catherine de Médicis, who wished to question this new star in the French prophetic firmament. An inveterate occultist, she was in the habit of 'collecting' astrologers and magicians rather like stamps or cigarette-cards, and clearly the new prophet of Provence could not be allowed to escape her net.

And so the seer set out in late June 1555 and, travelling via Lyon (where he confessed to a premonition that he might shortly be beheaded), reached Paris as early as mid-August thanks to having the royal post-horse network placed at his disposal. The Queen, clearly, could not wait to see the new phenomenon.

Q. Don't some commentators insist that he was summoned to Paris the *following* year, 1556?

A. This is simply a case of one author getting the wrong idea, then everybody else copying it. It arises from one rather ambiguous statement made by the prophet's son, César Nostradamus, in his *Histoire et Chronique de Provence* of 1614. All the other evidence, including dated private correspondence, shows that the visit in fact took place in 1555 – the Queen having presumably already received for the royal library, hot off the presses, the copy of the new book that was required under a statute of the former King François I.

The morning after he arrived in Paris Nostradamus was whisked out to the royal summer residence at the castle of St-Germain-en-Laye by the High Constable in person, the strangely named Anne de Montmorency – at least according to César's much later and possibly embroidered account. There, after being presented to King Henri II, he was interviewed at length by the Queen before being taken back to Paris, where he was installed in his temporary quarters at the town residence of the powerful Archbishop of Sens, Cardinal Louis de Bourbon.

Q. Isn't the Queen supposed to have questioned him at

length on his prediction at *Century* I, verse 35, that the
King would be killed in a duel?

A. Nothing is known about the content of the interview.

No sooner was the seer safely installed, however, than he
suffered a severe attack of gout (an illness which was to
plague him for the rest of his life) and was incapacitated for
nearly a fortnight. Possibly he had been plied with too much
fine wine. However, he put the setback to advantage by
making himself available for consultations by the nobility and
– it goes without saying – charging good money for them.

Once recovered, he was despatched by the Queen from
Paris to the royal castle at Blois, where he was instructed to
examine the seven royal children currently in residence there
both physically and astrologically for signs of their future
prospects. He was reportedly taken aback both by their
astrological prospects and by their tubercular constitutions
and, on returning to Paris, would (reportedly) tell the
Queen no more than 'All your sons will be kings'. He was
suitably rewarded for his pains.

However, the Justices of Paris, aware that the new-found
seer had now been added to the flood of astrologers and
magicians with whom the city was currently awash, seem to
have chosen this moment to launch an investigation into him.
Forewarned, the seer did his usual trick of leaving in a hurry
and set off on the long journey back home. So, at least, he
would later write to one Jean Morel (who had lent him
money to pay his hotel bill on his arrival) by way of
explaining why he had never got around to repaying him at
the time.

A likely story, you may think. But then, it may merely
have been a tale that he concocted to explain his sudden

disappearance from court in order to escape the Queen's over-eager clutches . . .

And so it was back to Salon again, trailing borrowed clouds of royal glory. The local citizens apparently celebrated him on his arrival as the most famous prophet in the whole of France. So now, perhaps, he could settle back into his normal routine and finish the job on which he was now firmly and irrevocably embarked.

3

Fame and Fortune

All the evidence suggests that Nostradamus now got on with the rest of his planned book of world prophecies at top speed. By November 1557 he had reached at least verse 40 of the VIIth *Century*. We know this because the second edition of his work, published by Antoine du Rosne of Lyon in that month, finished with this verse. There was every sign, though, that the book had been prepared in a hurry. The presentation was skimpy, the typesetting crude, the punctuation mechanical and rudimentary (in all probability, such matters as punctuation were entirely in the printer's hands anyway). And this despite signs that the source-text had been corrected personally by Nostradamus, who is known to have been in Lyon at the time.

Not for the first time an author had discovered that type-setters, in correcting one mistake, often made three. Not for the first time, either, an edition of his prophecies had comprised a distinctly odd number of verses, probably for the same reasons as before.

Q. I thought that the VIIth *Century* finished at verse 42, or even 44?

A. Not originally. Verses 41 and 42 may have been part of the original manuscript, but numbers 43 and 44 were added – along with nearly two dozen other 'extra verses' – some years later, after the prophet's death.

The reason for the evident haste and carelessness may be that, in the wake of the dramatic military disaster at St-Quentin in August of that year (when the French army was heavily defeated and the city taken by Imperial troops with huge numbers of dead and wounded) it was felt that some kind of 'special' publication was needed to reflect what looked like the 'end of the world' for France.

But it was emphatically not the end of the world for Nostradamus. He simply carried on working. As a result, he had the whole collection of a thousand prophecies complete by June 1558. Indeed, the final instalment comprising the VIIIth, IXth and Xth *Centuries* is reported to have been published that very same year, along with a flattering covering letter to his patron, King Henri II, in which he explained and justified his methods and summarised some of his conclusions.

However, this publication seems to have provoked a barrage of criticism. At all events, it was at about this time that he started to be subjected to even more violent attacks than usual, especially from the French Protestant faction. These criticisms ranged from poisonous little two-liners (playing on the fact that *nostra damus* means 'We peddle quackeries' in Latin) to whole pamphlets directed at an alleged fraud and sorcerer by the name of Monstradamus (sic). In the course of them he was called everything from a liar, via a brainless blockhead, to a criminal charlatan. When a translation of his 1559 *Almanach* appeared in England the following year, he was attacked all over again with equal relish. And when, in 1560, the famous poet Pierre de Ronsard was bold enough to publish a pseudo-sonnet extolling the prophet, he was immediately tarred with the same brush, notwithstanding the fact that his eulogy was (as my published translation suggests) a quite carefully balanced one:

> Be it Great God beyond all space and time
> Roused Nostradamus' rapture into rhyme;
> Be he by daemon good or evil stirred,
> Or gifted with a soul that like some bird
> Soars up to heavens no mortal man may know
> To bring back auguries for us below;
> Be his a mind so gloomy, dark and dim,
> Crammed with gross humours, as to cozen him —
> Whate'er he is, he is: yet none the less
> Through the vague portents that his words express
> Like some old oracle he has foretold
> For many a year what fate for us shall hold.
>> I'd doubt him, did not heaven, that disburses
>> Both good and ill to men, inform his verses.

By this time, however, fate had intervened. After the defeat at St-Quentin, a peace had been signed under whose terms the leading Imperial general, Duke Emmanuel-Philibert of Savoy, would marry the King's sister, Marguerite de Valois, while Henri's daughter Elisabeth would marry King Philip II of Spain by proxy. The festivities were arranged for the end of June 1559. There were all the customary junketings, but the high-point was a jousting match between the King and the somewhat reluctant young Captain of his Scottish Guard,

one Gabriel de Lorge, Count of Montgomery. After two
indecisive jousts the King insisted on a third, ignoring the fact
that Scaliger's former mentor, the Italian magician and
astrologer Luca Gaurico, had long ago written to warn Henri
against 'all single combat in an enclosed space, especially
during his 41st year'.

The King having been born in 1519, this was indeed his
41st year.

Things went badly wrong. Montgomery's lance splintered
on impact and, penetrating the King's visor, entered his eye
and pierced his brain. He died in agony 11 days later.

At once the country was thrown into a ferment of fear and
uncertainty. With this strong central figure gone and only the
weak, adolescent, mother-dominated princes to succeed him,
the stage was finally set for the religious and civil war that
everybody knew was already brewing in the wings to break
out into the open and devastate the kingdom. Once again,
France seemed to be facing the end of everything.

What on earth would happen next?

It is at such times that astrologers and seers traditionally
come into their own. And, with the prophecies of the
favourite court prophet Nostradamus just completed and his
Almanachs still the rage, there was clearly only one person to
turn to ...

In no time at all the entire court was swept by rabid
Nostradamania. Foreign ambassadors were soon reporting
home in terms suggesting that, for the moment at least, no
rational negotiations were possible with people so obsessed.
The *Propheties* were avidly scanned for indications of the fate
of Henri's successor, the 16-year-old François II and
his only slightly older wife, Mary Queen of Scots.
Nostradamus's publication of a further work designed to
warn everybody of the malign effects of the major eclipse due

on 16 September that year merely made matters worse.

The royal tragedy, in short, had finally made Nostradamus's name – not necessarily because he had predicted it, but because he was the right man in the right place at the right time.

Q. But I thought he *had* predicted it, in verse I.35?

> *The younger lion shall surmount the old*
> *On martial field in duel man-to-man.*
> *Twice challenged, thrice; eyes pierced in cage of gold,*
> *Death shall come hard as only dying can.*

A. Possibly he had. Yet there is no actual evidence that anybody at the time thought so. The first person to suggest it in print was Nostradamus's son César, writing in 1614, all of 55 years later. Even the seer's own secretary, Jean de Chavigny, seems not to have heard of the idea.

As for the seer himself, he did claim to have predicted it, but in a different verse entirely. Writing three years later to one Jean de Vauzelles, he complimented him on his ability to uncloak the underlying meaning of his obscure language, quoting specifically the verse that read: *Lors que un oeil en France regnera, Et quant le grain de Bloys son amy tuera* ...

This is clearly a reference to verse III.55, which reads, in translation:

> *The year that France the one-eyed govern will,*
> *The Court shall be immersed in grievous trouble:*
> *The Lord of Blois his bosom-friend shall kill,*
> *The realm consigned to doubt and evil double.*

But the seer had obviously quoted it imperfectly, probably from memory – a fact which had conveniently allowed him to write *le grain* ('the grain') instead of line 3's original *le grand* ('the Great One, or Lord'), to fit the fact that Montgomery's name, 'Lorge', was actually the French for 'barley' (*l'orge*) . . .

No doubt the error was unintentional (!). But all too often similar squirmings are made by would-be seers who, over-anxious to prove their prophetic credentials, retrospectively twist their predictions to fit events.

Could Nostradamus, one wonders, have been one such?

At one and the same time, though, the disaster had placed Nostradamus himself in 'grievous trouble'. How was it, after all, that only a year previously he had blithely dedicated his final instalment to the King, apparently without either realising that the latter would shortly cease to exist, or even warning him of imminent danger? What sort of a court prophet was that?

Besides, if he now proposed to issue his omnibus edition of all one thousand prophecies, he would have to write a new dedication – presumably to the new King François. No doubt the admirable Jean de Tournes, who had published his last instalment in Paris, would allow him to do so. But would he also be able to recover from Antoine du Rosne of Lyon the 60 verses of *Century* VII that the latter had omitted to publish in the original second instalment, apparently on the assumption that he himself would be including them in the final one?

The signs are that he was unable to. Possibly Du Rosne stood on what he assumed to be his rights. Having duly returned to Nostradamus the manuscript sheets for verses I.1

to VII.42 (thus allowing the addition of the as yet unpublished VII.41 and VII.42), perhaps he simply refused to hand over the rest. Certainly something of the kind must have happened, for no further edition appeared during the seer's lifetime, and the last 58 verses of the VIIth century remained unpublished even when the final, omnibus edition did eventually come out in 1568, two years after his death.

For, Nostradamus being his usual, vague self, he had no doubt mislaid his own copy ...

There was nothing to be done, then, but to carry on with his other work. There were various bits of academic translation and commentary waiting to be completed. There were 58 new prophecies to be prepared, to replace the 58 'lost' ones of *Century* VII. And so, apparently at some point after 1561, the *Sixains* came into being, to be discovered among the seer's papers only after his death (together with another couple of dozen quatrains that were probably discarded drafts).

Q. I thought the *Sixains* were supposed to be forgeries, with a style nothing like that of the *Centuries*?

A. They are indeed different, though their style is not quite so dissimilar to that of some of the later *Présages*, and aspects of the symbolism seem to be related to that of another of his books, the *Orus Apollo*. Their internal dates and details, too, seem to fit in with those of the other prophecies.

But then the stylistic argument is liable to backfire anyway. Anybody attempting to *forge* Nostradamian prophecies would have been likely to stick as closely as possible to the original style and format. Anything else would have been a dead giveaway.

The only 'forger' confident enough to replace the seer's familiar dense four-liners with much more airy six-liners, in other words, is likely to have been Nostradamus himself.

Then there were the *Almanachs* to continue with. True, publishing them was becoming increasingly dangerous. So influential were they that, in the present uncertain climate, their political and military predictions were quite liable to act as triggers for new religious and constitutional upheavals. In view of this, in January 1561 an edict was issued forbidding the writers of almanacs (which, of course, meant nobody if not Nostradamus!) to issue their publications until they had been checked and approved by a bishop. But the seer was either too vague or too vain to take any notice either of the new rule or of the friends who wrote to him urging caution, and in November he published his 1562 *Almanach* regardless. Nostradamus was arrested and imprisoned in the castle of Marignane by the Governor of Provence. However, when the latter asked what he should do next, no very terrible punishment seems to have been demanded, for the seer was quickly released again.

Perhaps it was not too surprising. He had, after all, only just supplied the King himself with his royal birthchart and commentary. And besides, the Governor was one of his oldest and closest friends – namely Claude, Duke of Tende.

Q. Didn't Nostradamus also write the so-called prophecies of Orval?

A. No – neither those of Orval (in the Ardennes), nor the related prophecies of Olivarius, nor the multitude of anonymous 'Orval' prophecies that have supposedly been unearthed since. The two original collections, dated '1542', are fairly obvious forgeries composed at the end of the 18th century in studiedly antique (but totally un-Nostradamian) style to celebrate Napoleon – who, predictably perhaps, assumed that they were genuine. Those that have surfaced since are, on the basis of their style and vocabulary, no less dubious in origin.

Moreover, in view of the fact that the Ardennes region was a war-zone between France to the west and the Empire to the east at the time, the likelihood that scholarly travellers such as Nostradamus were anywhere near Orval in 1542 is remote in the extreme.

Having long since become the talk of the town, Nostradamus was now approached by everybody who was anybody for consultations and horoscopes. The late King's sister had already visited him in Salon on the way back from the funeral to her new home in Savoy. After the young King François's early death, the Queen herself visited him in 1564 with her son, the new King Charles IX. During the visit, the ageing seer is even alleged to have 'discovered' among their huge retinue the young Protestant Prince of Navarre who would subsequently become the great King Henri IV and finally bring the Wars of Religion to an end. To crown it all, he was appointed Privy Councillor and official Physician-in-Ordinary to the King, and given a pension to match.

Whether or not this occasion has anything to do with the subject-matter of the 'death quatrain' quoted on p. 12, Nostradamus now seems to have been virtually on his last legs. Increasingly plagued by gout and arthritis, he struggled on for another year-and-a-half, then – having at the last moment drawn up a will that left virtually all his considerable fortune to his wife in trust for his six children – finally succumbed to dropsy (oedema) in the early hours of Sunday, 2 July 1566. They reportedly found him, barely cold, slumped on the floor between his bed and the bench that he had had placed alongside it – apparently just as the verse had predicted.

He was buried, as he had requested, in the left-hand wall of Salon's Franciscan chapel, not far outside the town's north gate. He was granted full civic honours, and his tomb was marked by a plaque bearing a fulsome Latin inscription allegedly composed by the now 12-year-old César.

Soon this spot, sacred to the one 'who alone of all mortals was judged worthy to describe with near-divine pen the events of the whole world under the influence of the stars', would become a place of recognised public veneration. Only at the time of the French Revolution, when the chapel had fallen into disuse and ruin, were his remains first unearthed by drunken soldiers, then scattered among the population, and finally recovered and re-entombed in the chapel of Our Lady (in the language of the time, *Nostre Dame!*) in the nearby church of St-Laurent, where they remain to this day.

Q. Wasn't he buried upright, with a medallion around his neck spelling out the exact date when he would be dug up?

A. No. Unfortunately there is no historical evidence for either story.

Q. What about his original burial site? Has the Franciscan chapel totally disappeared?

A. No, you can still visit a part of it that is incorporated into the restaurant *La Brocherie* in the rue Hozier, provided you are prepared to buy a meal there! You will not find his original tomb, though.

4

The Prophetic Legacy

For the last 400 years and more the 1,141 'Official' Prophecies have hardly ever been out of print. During all that time, too, they have never ceased to work their magic.

Some have regarded them with contempt, or even apathy. Others – possibly the majority – have regarded them with a mixture of awe, fear and credulity. Every generation has sought to read into them the events and expectations of its own time, often twisting their words unmercifully in the process. Editors have often assisted in this, changing the seer's words and spellings from what they actually said to what they thought they *ought* to have said. Whole books have been written, and false expectations raised, on the basis of such corrupt editions. And unscrupulous politicians and war-leaders have deliberately used them to justify their acts, sometimes even commissioning new, fake ones for purposes of propaganda.

Q. Is it true, as the *Encyclopaedia Britannica* states, that they were placed on the *Index of Forbidden Books* by the Vatican's Congregation of the Index in 1781?

A. *Britannica* also states that there were 20 editions of the *Index*. Extensive research has been carried out by Michel Chomarat and his colleagues into *all 25 editions* at the Bibliothèque Municipale de Lyon. It turns out that in no edition of it is Nostradamus mentioned at all, even though various of his works are banned in the five Spanish/Flemish equivalents.

And there was no 1781 edition of either.

Meanwhile, would-be scholars have sought hidden formulae to unscramble their order. Others have devised special decoding techniques in an attempt to make sense of the words. Foreigners have asserted that Nostradamus was really writing about their own countries, or even via their own languages.

Q. Surely there's plenty of evidence that Nostradamus *was* writing in code? Didn't he himself state that he deliberately used obscure language, and that people wouldn't be able to understand his prophecies?

A. He did indeed. But writing in obscure language – which he obviously does – doesn't necessarily mean writing in code. This, after all, was quite unnecessary, even if he had had the time to do so, since (just as he predicted) not too many people can make head or tail of his prophecies anyway. The fact that the prophecies *might just as well be* in code does not necessarily mean that they *are!*

Those who devise special codes for reading

Nostradamus and then apply them to his prophecies generally finish up by discovering in them not his ideas, but their own.

Only quite recently has French research in particular enabled scholars to identify the original texts and relate them to the seer's true cultural context, and so to establish on that basis what the seer is actually likely to have meant and how he is likely to have arrived at his conclusions. As yet the results have barely begun to filter through either to the commentators or to the public.

Consequently it has so far been virtually impossible to assess Nostradamus's prophecies with any degree of reliability. Neither in respect of their past accuracy, nor in respect of their future prospects, has it been possible to arrive at any firm conclusions. The general feeling among commentators that Nostradamus was perhaps 80 per cent accurate has been totally negated by the fact that no two commentators have been able to agree about the true meaning of any more than a handful of verses.

Now that the research has been done, however, what *can* be said about the seer's past accuracy? This, after all, has to condition our expectations about what to expect of his prophecies in the future.

Very few of the prophecies contain actual calendar dates. Yet unless a prophecy is dated it is virtually impossible to be sure either that it has been fulfilled or that it hasn't. In the first case it can only be said that this was just *one* of any number of possible fulfilments; in the second, that it hasn't happened *yet*. Biblical prophecies, particularly, are liable to be treated by keen Christians in this latter way.

There is only one other case where one can be virtually sure that a prophecy has been fulfilled — and that it is where it refers to some absolutely unique event, such as the first time that some particular thing happens in the history of the world.

How far, then, do Nostradamus's prophecies measure up to this? Less than a dozen of the prophecies are in fact dated in the normal way or are clearly date-related, while a further 17 of the *Sixains* also include what appear to be dates. Of the former:

I.62 refers via contemporary astrological lore to the year 1887, but was unsuccessful in that it predicted a serious decline in learning and literacy before then.

X.91 refers to the year 1609, and was nearly successful in that the contemporary Pope fell seriously ill instead of actually dying and being replaced in that year as apparently predicted.

X.100 successfully – and remarkably – predicts over 300 years of pre-eminence for a future empire ruled over by the then only second-class power that was England.

I.49 predicts for 1700 a major invasion of northern Europe by the Muslim Middle East that in fact never took place (but we have already noted Nostradamus's propensity to suggest this particular eventuality).

III.77 pinpoints October 1727 as a time when the king of Persia would be captured by the Egyptians – which chimes in vaguely (though far from exactly) with the fact that in that month the Shah of Persia handed over considerable territories to the Ottoman Turks, who ruled Egypt at the time.

The **Letter to Henri II** predicts with great accuracy that

1792 would see the birth of a completely new age or world order, as indeed happened with the final proclamation of the post-revolutionary French Republic in that year – though, to be fair, astrologers had, it seems, been predicting some sort of upheaval in or around 1789 (the year of the Revolution itself) for at least a century before Nostradamus.

Q. What about VI.54 and VIII.71? Is it true, as some commentators suggest, that their shared date of '1607' is meant to be counted either in months from the birth of Hitler in 1889 or in years from the Council of Nicea in AD 325?

A. No, this is a bit of a red herring, since Nostradamus makes it clear that in these cases he is using a different count entirely, apparently tied to the foundation of the Christian liturgy in AD 392. The date referred to, in other words, is in fact 1999.

As for the *Sixains*, 17 of them mention a range of dates between '604 and '670. If these are meant to be references to the 1600s, virtually all the predictions involved turned out to be abject failures. However, there is some evidence that these dates, too, are meant to refer to the foundation of the Church's liturgy, and so still lie for the most part a few years into our future.

This leaves, then, only those predictions that refer to events so obvious and unique that all the commentators are forced to agree on them. Among these, Sixain 52 cannot but refer to the notorious St Bartholomew's Day massacre of 1572, when the young King Charles IX, apparently at the behest of his formidable mother Queen Catherine de Médicis, attempted to wipe out the Protestant faction by massacring most of its

leaders overnight. In my earlier translation in *Nostradamus –
The Next 50 Years* this reads:

> Another blow, great town, half-starved anew
> The feast of blessed Saint Bartholomew
> Shall grave into the bowels of your heart.
> At Nîmes, Rochelle, Geneva, Montpellier,
> Castres and Lyon, Mars on his Arian way
> Shall wager all on noble lady's part.

Another evident bull's-eye is the prediction at IX.49 that
England's parliament would put its King to death – an event
which has happened only once so far, with the beheading of
Charles I in 1649:

> Brussels and Ghent shall march against Anvers
> And London's parliament its king shall slay.
> Wine shall be ta'en for wit: confusion there,
> With government in deepest disarray.

Q. Don't Erika Cheetham and others also say that
quatrain II.51 refers to the Fire of London?

A. Yes, I have reported this claim myself. But in fact it is
based on a highly dubious reading of Nostradamus's *de
vingt trois les six* in line 2, which on the face of it means
not 'of three score and six' (i.e. '66), as Erika Cheetham
contends, but simply 'six out of twenty-three'.

Similar claims – notably by Cheetham and John
Hogue – that dates are sometimes encoded in the
verse-numbers (as in the case of IX.49 above) are no
less appealing, but are sufficiently consistent to
suggest this as a valid dating technique.

Even more impressive, however, is Nostradamus's prediction in the Letter to Henri II of an October revolution – he actually calls it a *translation* or 'transfer', presumably of power – whose effects will last for 73 years and 7 months, while the Church will be renewed by a figure from the 50th degree of latitude. The October Revolution of 1917 in Russia did indeed produce a regime which lasted until the summer of 1991 – almost exactly 73 years and 7 months later – and at this very same time Pope John Paul II was managing to renew and reinvigorate the Church, especially in Poland, where he had formerly been Archbishop of Cracow, a city which lies at 50° 03' North!

The Romanian commentator Vlaicu Ionescu was even canny enough to spot the first of these links beforehand and consequently to predict the event. His sales, particularly in Japan, benefited accordingly.

Then there is the celebrated 'Varennes' prophecy at IX.20, which begs to be identified with the attempted flight abroad of Louis XVI and his Queen, Marie-Antoinette, in June 1792, during the latter stages of the French Revolution. My fairly free translation in *Nostradamus – The Next 50 Years* reads:

> *Through woods of Reims by night shall make her way*
> *Herne the white butterfly, by byways sent.*
> *The elected head, Varennes's black monk in grey*
> *Sows storm, fire, blood and foul dismemberment.*

However exact or inexact the translation, the fact remains that the details more or less fit, and that virtually nothing else of importance is ever known to have happened at Varennes.

Similarly unique, of course, is the British royal abdication due to matters matrimonial that appears to be signalled by X.22:

For lack of will to let divorcing be
Which aftertimes unworthy should be deemed,
The Islands' king shall be constrained to flee,
Replaced by one who never kingly seemed.

The details would seem to fit like a glove the celebrated abdication of Edward VIII in 1936 in order to marry the American divorcee Mrs Wallis Simpson, followed by the accession of his shy and unwilling brother who would become George VI.

And finally, VIII.70 seems to fit the Gulf War of 1991 so exactly as to make it possible to date this quatrain, too:

Wicked and vile, a man of ill repute,
The tyrant of Iraq comes in apace.
With Babylon's Great Whore all plead their suit.
Horrid the land shall be, and black its face.

On top of this, Nostradamus appears to mention by name Napoleon at VIII.1, Franco at IX.16, De Gaulle possibly at IX.33, Pasteur just as possibly at I.25 – and these identifications, if valid, would likewise tend to fix the dates of the verses in which they appear.

Q. Doesn't Nostradamus also name Chirac and Hitler?

A. No. One or two commentators and quite a lot of French people have naturally jumped on the 'Chirac' bandwagon, but (this apart) it has always been assumed – even by the seer's own secretary – that the name 'Chyren' (mentioned in six different verses) is an anagram for 'Henryc', and thus a reference to the long-awaited future Henri V of France. Nostradamus even capitalises the name, apparently in order to draw our attention to the fact, just as he does with a variety of other 'unusual' words that are clearly anagrams. There is little in common between this glorious young conquering hero, whom Nostradamus seems to represent as saving Europe during the early years of the next century, and the somewhat elderly French President who is so prone to shoot himself in the foot.

As for Hitler, the name 'Hiʃter' *is* mentioned three times – at II.24, IV.68 and V.29 – but the context nearly always makes it perfectly clear that the reference is not to the Austro-German dictator, whose name looks rather similar, but to the river Danube, of which it was the name in classical times, when it and the Rhine (which is also mentioned in the first two cases) formed the north-eastern frontier of the Roman empire. Two further references at *Présages* 15 and 31, this time without the 'H' (and dated for 1557 and 1558 respectively!), tend to confirm this.

But apart from these few cases, the identification of past fulfilments is so much a matter of chance and personal preference that few commentators can ever agree on them. No doubt this is because we are once again in the familiar territory of trying retrospectively to fit events to prophecies, rather than the other way around. This has always proved difficult for enthusiasts to resist. It is all too tempting, after all, to stretch a meaning here or slightly adjust a word there in order to get a verse to say what you want it to say in the light of what you already know.

So that, in the end what one discovers is always what one *wants* to discover, rather than what is actually there.

Q. Isn't it true that you can make Nostradamus's prophecies mean anything you like?

A. Precisely — all the while you insist on taking each prophecy in isolation. Much the same can apply if you insist on treating individual verses of the Bible in a similar way. Taken out of context, almost any statement can be made to mean many things, and it is for this reason that the establishment of *context* is a vital prerequisite for any translation or interpretation of Nostradamus. Merely hooking up isolated verses with isolated incidents as the fancy takes you — and especially the latest major crisis or disaster — simply will not do, and threatens totally to misrepresent what he actually said and meant.

But then this tendency to read preconceived ideas into the *Prophecies* not only bedevils people's attempts to identify fulfilled Nostradamian predictions from the past, but completely undermines any objective attempt to assess what Nostradamus predicts for our future, too.

What we need, in other words, is some technique for anticipating the future on the basis of Nostradamus's prophecies that does *not* involve reading them in the light of our own prejudices and prior assumptions — some technique that will free us just as much from biblical eschatology on the one hand as from common science-fiction extrapolations on the other, to say nothing of our own ordinary, everyday, commonsense expectations, which are, in the event, liable to be just as misleading.

And the key to any such technique has, as indicated above, to be *context* — the context, that is, within which Nostradamus actually wrote his prophecies, rather than the context within which we may now choose to read them.

5

The Shape of Things to Come

Context is essential to the understanding not merely of language, but of events too. An event has its true meaning only in what leads up to it and what results from it. The Russian Revolution, for example, is largely meaningless other than in terms of what it did to the previous regime and what kind of regime it went on to produce – to say nothing of all the international consequences in the form of the defeat of Hitler, the communisation of Eastern Europe, the Cold War, the nuclear arms race and so on. The death of Hitler, too, is significant mainly in terms of the terrors that went before it and the new Europe – indeed, the new world – to which it was eventually to lead.

Nostradamus's prophecies, similarly, are almost meaningless in isolation. If they refer to real events as they unfold, then they too must inevitably mirror both the historical antecedents and the historical after-effects that are associated with those events. They too, in other words, must have a logical sequence which gives them meaning and relevance, even if Nostradamus himself may not have been aware of that sequence when he was writing them.

Q. Isn't it true, then, that he deliberately scrambled the order of his prophecies?

A. Probably not. It would have been quite unnecessary. Their disordered sequence seems much more likely to have been the natural result of the way in which he composed them — which will be examined later.

Naturally, though, the resultant organisational chaos suited his purposes down to the ground. It all helped, after all, to ensure that what he was saying was not so clear as to provoke his enemies, nor so obvious as to risk being proved wrong. Besides, he may have been all too aware of the dangers of self-fulfilment if his prophecies were too clearly understood.

Aside from the dated verses, then, it is the sequencing of Nostradamus's prophecies that alone can guide us towards the true meaning of any single one of them — and even in the case of the dated verses, no final meaning can be established until the sequencing has been done.

In order to understand the role of any one piece of the jigsaw-puzzle, we must first patiently reconstruct the picture on the box.

Where Nostradamus's prophecies for our future are concerned, then, we have to start by establishing whatever dates we can, then sequence the remaining verses around the resulting framework.

At first sight, admittedly, the prospects for establishing future dates look slim, since he gives only two clear calendar dates for our future. One is the year 3797, which he gives in his preface as the terminal year for his prophecies. The other is the seventh month of 1999, which is mentioned in the now-notorious verse X.72.

What the French actually says is:

> *L'an mil neuf cens nonante neuf sept mois*
> *Du ciel viendra un grand Roy deffraieur*
> *Resusciter le grand Roy d'Angolmois.*
> *Avant apres Mars regner par bon heur.*

and most commentators have seen in it warnings of a great 'King of Terror' – the long-awaited Antichrist, no less – who will descend from the skies to resurrect Genghis Khan and initiate Armageddon. In fact, though, the verse says nothing about a King of Terror (capitalised or otherwise), mentions no Antichrist, does not necessarily mean that whoever it is will come from the sky, says nothing about Genghis Khan and is entirely innocent of any suggestion of Armageddon.

Such, unfortunately, are the almost inevitable results of incompetent, amateurish translation compounded by frankly tendentious interpretation.

For a start, *un grand Roy deffraieur* means 'a great defraying King' – i.e. one who pays up or even appeases (the variant *d'effraieur* – 'of fear' – appears only in relatively corrupt later editions). Again, while *Angolmois* could conceivably be an anagram of *Mongolois*, it could equally well refer to a latter-day François I, whose dukedom was the area of Angoumois. As for lines 2 and 3, closer analysis of the verse's syntax in fact suggests that they are merely a typical 'Virgilian' version of '*un grand Roy du ciel deffraieur viendra resusciter le grand Roy d'Angolmois*' – which merely suggests that a great heavenly king with a desire to appease and/or money to spend will once more stir up a great king from Angoumois (or, just conceivably, the great King of the Mongols). The most likely 'heavenly king' being the Pope, then, my most recent suggested translation of the verse (from my *Nostradamus Encyclopedia*) reads:

> *When 1999 is seven months o'er*
> *Shall heaven's great Vicar, anxious to appease*
> *Stir up the Mongol-Lombard King once more,*
> *And war reign haply where it once did cease.*

But then this version also comes courtesy of further research, this time into the comparative horoscopy underlying the verse (see Chapter 7) – which in fact identifies the figure in question as another Pope Gregory the Great, and moreover (in its most recently calculated version) places the meeting of the two leaders at the latitude of Sarajevo.

As for the verse's ostensible dating, Nostradamus's 'seventh month', on the then current Julian calendar, works out at 14 July to 13 August on our current Gregorian one.

Q. Couldn't this be based on the fact that there is a major solar eclipse due on 11 August 1999? As for the 'King of Terror from the sky', I'm sure I read recently that this is actually a comet or asteroid that is destined to crash into the Earth, causing widespread devastation and conflict. Shouldn't I believe this?

A. Not unless you also believe that Nostradamus couldn't tell the difference between a man and a mountain. In all other cases, after all, *roy* means 'king', and comets are signified by words such as *comete* or *astre crinite* ('hairy star', which is what the original Greek word *kometes* actually means). The seer happily uses both. Quite why his words should suddenly take on totally changed and unknown meanings in this particular verse alone is something that nobody has managed to explain – other than because it would help to back up their own personal hopes or expectations.

As for the solar eclipse, it is highly unlikely that Nostradamus's tables were accurate enough to predict so fleeting a phenomenon so far in advance – though it is not entirely impossible, of course, that he did manage to foresee it by other means (see Chapter 8).

Two dated verses, then, plus up to 19 further verses (VI.54 and VIII.71, plus 17 of the *Sixains*) that can possibly be dated by counting from the foundation of the Church's liturgy in AD 392 – this, clearly, is not much to go on.

But then Nostradamus also gives us two or three dozen astrological references which can likewise help date the particular verses concerned – even though, in the nature of things, astrological configurations tend to come around again and again. At V.25, for example, he predicts that an 'Arab lord' whom he describes as a 'coiled snake', and who is destined to overwhelm Christendom by sea, will invade Turkey and Egypt with around a million men when Mars, Venus and the sun are in Leo.

This configuration in fact occurs next in August 1998.

By the time you read this, therefore, you will have a fair idea of whether either the prediction or its next possible astrological dating is correct. Failing that, you will have to wait until August 2015 to make a new assessment, since that is when this particular pattern will next repeat itself.

Datewise, then, that seems to be about the size of it – 40 or 50 datable verses at most. Yet there is a further possibility. Basic to Nostradamus's method as we shall see, was the calculation of the dates when known historical events ought to repeat themselves – a calculation based on when the astrological patterns obtaining at the time were destined to come around again. It ought therefore to be possible, by identifying those original events, to carry out the same calculations as he did, and so arrive at the same dates. He claimed in his covering Letter to King Henri II, after all, that he was perfectly capable of dating *all* his quatrains – and it follows that, if *he* could, *we* should be able to do so, too. On this basis, then, the number of datable verses is limited only by our knowledge of ancient history and our ability to spot those same ancient events as are mirrored in the seer's verses.

I have in fact already carried out over two dozen such calculations, each resulting in a pair of charts which I call *horographs* – one showing the planetary positions at the time of the original event, the other showing the equivalent positions for the theoretical future event, along with a selection of possibly relevant verses. These data are clearly set out in my *Nostradamus Encyclopedia*. As a result, we can possibly add a further couple of dozen datable verses to our count – making a total so far of perhaps seventy, or even more.

However, this is only a beginning, since Nostradamus appears to write his verses *in pairs*. True, it has not yet been possible to establish this as a universal principle, but the fact that the very first two clearly form such a pair could be seen as suggesting this principle at the outset, and it is not at all difficult to spot (on the basis of their detailed content) a whole range of other 'pairs' too, even though the verses involved are in most cases widely separated.

In theory, then, it is only necessary to discover the 'pairs' of our datable verses so far to increase our total to a possible 140 or so.

Now this is not a bad proportion. With an overall total of some 1,141 prophecies, it amounts to more than 12 per cent. And, on top of this, Nostradamus helps us out with a whole range of summary-verses, just as he did in the *Présages*.

At X.100, for example, he paints a 300-year future for the British Empire that is presumably based on the story of some earlier, as-yet-unidentified equivalent, redated by reference to the relevant astrological cycles and displaced only in the matter of latitude. At *Présage* 40 and *Century* IV.50 he warns that a massive oriental invasion of Europe will not be beaten back until seven rulers in turn have ruled over it — a notion no doubt borrowed once again from ancient history. At XII.36 (one of the 'extra' quatrains), VI.80 and V.68 he paints a similar picture, no doubt based on earlier invasions by the Moors and Ottomans, to say nothing of the classical Hannibal. At IX.55 and VII.34 he describes the invasion's awful effects in terms of disease and privation, especially in France, and at V.13 not only the invasion itself, but its eventual defeat.

While all of these future developments are presumably datable in terms of comparative horoscopy (see Chapter 7), the fact remains that the summary verses concerned are designed to cover long periods of time, and so can hopefully serve as general templates for our reconstruction of the future that Nostradamus foresees for us.

And it has to be said that the looming Muslim invasion seems to be by far the major theme, as far as the years immediately ahead are concerned, notwithstanding the fact that Nostradamus has, as we have already seen, been wrong about it in the past ...

At the time of writing, my own assessment of the *datable* prophecies for the future (based largely on my *Nostradamus: The Final Reckoning* and *Nostradamus Encyclopedia*, which offers full explanations and details of verse numbers) thus runs as follows:

1998 Possible coronation of British King or inauguration of American President (June/July).

Middle Eastern Muslim powers prepare to invade Turkey and Egypt (August).

Western Turkey threatened by sea.

Ever more violent anti-European activities by Arab nationalists and/or North African Muslims.

Chancellor 'as big as an ox' pays last visit to Paris before leaving office (but see 2001).

1999 Huge invasion of Turkey and Aegean by 'another Xerxes' from Iran.

France and Italy start to be threatened by the above invasion (February).

Further increase in North African anti-European activities.

King of Morocco overthrown and imprisoned by pan-Arabic revolution.

Astrologers multiply, but are persecuted and their books banned (presumably in France).

Pope travels to Sarajevo to buy off Middle Eastern invaders, but merely succeeds in stirring the pot (July/August).

'Mongol' hordes invade south-eastern Europe and Balkans.

Start of Antichrist's reign.

European Union over-confident only a year or so before its final collapse.

Re-emergence of British 'Joan of Arc' figure.

Muslim seaborne forces invade Sicily.

2000 A 'new Nebuchadnezzar' from Iraq invades Egypt, in alliance with forces from further west.

Asiatic forces invade Armenia.

European navies beat off a larger Muslim fleet off Sicily.

Muslims from Turkey invade south-eastern Italy.

Pope forced to flee Italy by Asiatic invasion; comet appears (October?).

Pope dies near Lyon France; comet disappears (December?).

2001 Alternative date for ox-like Chancellor's last visit to Paris.

New Pope elected, destined to betray the Church (January or March).

2002 Islamic forces victorious in Italy and Greece (May).

War resumes in Italy (June onwards).

Rome under renewed attack.

Alien forces plunder Italy.

Asiatics overrun Sinai and Egypt.

Invaders start to look towards France.

Violent attack on France from the sea.

2003 War-conference of invading commanders near Venice.

North African Muslims overwhelm Malta and Gibraltar.

2004 Drought in the south.

Severe earthquakes and tidal waves in eastern Mediterranean wreak vast destruction in Greece, Turkey and even Italy (August).

Southern and western European economies collapse (December).

The Church in flames; plague and captivity.
Muslim forces attack Lyon and the Gironde estuary.

2005   Volcanic ash or 'fire from the sky' over southern Europe.
Invading forces withdraw to central Italy to recuperate (March).
Last Pope ejected from office.

2006   Local Italian leader murdered at Fossano on orders from Rome (February).

2007   Beginning of window for birth of Henri V, future King of France and saviour of Europe (May?).
Western navies abandon Mediterranean: Asiatic invasion resumes via North Africa, Balearics and Spain (September).
France under renewed attack.
Death of France begins.

2009   Anti-European violence by North African Muslims reaches its peak.
Blue-turbaned Muslim leader invades south-western France.

2010   Further Muslim forces attack Hungary and southern France.

2011   'New Cyrus the Great' burns Rome and executes Pope.
Huge epidemic devastates France.

2012   End of window for birth of Henri V of France.

Further epidemic hits France.
Final death-knell tolls for France.

2013 First spearhead of Muslim invaders penetrates south-western France via Pyrenees (January/February).
'Fire from the sky' over southern Europe, and especially south-western France.
Muslim 'creeping bombardment' of northern Europe begins.
Possible death from illness of major Asiatic leader.

2014 Last Pope murdered in captivity (August).

2015 Rome sacked; Vatican burned.
South-western France attacked with thermal weapons: Garonne defence-line overrun (July/August).

2017 Muslim invaders cross Pyrenees in force, armed with chemical weapons (January).
Aerial attacks prove the last straw for France.
South-western France attacked with thermal weapons: Garonne defence-line overrun (July/August – alternative date).
Narbonne falls to the Muslims (December).

2019 Rome reinvaded by North Africans.
Possible death of second Middle Eastern leader.

2021 Muslim invaders reach Luxembourg and a flooded Lorraine (February).

2022 Muslim overlord officially installed at Reims and Aix-la-Chapelle (Aachen); Asiatic empire reaches its furthest extent on Belgian border and English Channel coast (February); biological attacks on Britain from the air.

2022 Severe epidemic hits France: up to two-thirds of population and livestock eventually wiped out (March).

2025 Reinvasion and liberation of France by combined Western forces based in Germany and Britain.

2026 Assassination of Asiatic overlord; his empire divided. France, *in extremis*, finally liberated (April).

2027 Counter-invasion of Italy.

2028 Northern allies back in control of both France and Italy.
French leader assumes supreme power in Europe (November).

2031 A third Asiatic leader drowned or burnt to death.

2032 New, young French leader – the future Henri V – marries; floods in France.
Allies strike fear into North African leader.
Franco-Italian civil war begins (June?).

2034 Allied forces end propaganda war and sweep into southern Spain (January/February).
Muslim invaders finally expelled from Spain.
Beginning of 57-year period of peace and prosperity.

2036 European forces attack Muslim Middle Eastern heart-lands via southern Turkey in 'new crusade'.

2044 Last likely date for beginning of above age of peace and prosperity.

2062 Final collapse of Asiatic empire in the East with death of 'Phoenix'.

2091 End of initial era of world peace and prosperity (?).

2828 Last Judgement; beginning of true Millennium (?).

3797 End of earthly Millennium; new, temporary period of growing troubles leading up to final Kingdom of Heaven (?).

To the extent that this summary is valid (and clearly I have not sought to justify it in any detail here), it provides a useful and quite detailed template around which to fit many of the remaining prophecies.

Q. What does Nostradamus have to say about Armageddon and the end of the world, then?

A. Nothing. He never mentions either idea.

6

Consulting the
Oracle

How, then, are you to find out exactly what Nostradamus said? You should never, after all, take anybody else's word for it – least of all mine. The whole subject is bedevilled by those who insist on waving around vague claims about what he predicted, often without even having read him.

They are rather like all those would-be biblical experts who insist on plying you with non-existent quotations from the Bible. 'You've got to eat a pound of dirt before you die', possibly. Or, more humorously, the bit about King David's noisy motorbike – 'And David's triumph was heard throughout the land'. Or, alas, the mistranslated 'Where there is no vision, the people perish.' Or even the much-revered and oft-quoted, but nevertheless bogus 'The kingdom of heaven is within you'.

Not one of them is in fact to be found anywhere in the original scriptures.

As with the Bible, so with Nostradamus. In both cases you need to stick closely to what the texts actually say if you don't want to be led up the garden path. And this involves actually going back to the originals.

But how?

There are two main plans of possible attack:

Plan A – Learn to Consult Them for Yourself

This is the safest and most straightforward option. However, there are a number of rather demanding prerequisites:

1. You will need to have a thorough knowledge of French. This means not just schoolboy or schoolgirl French, but French up to pre-university standard at least, and preferably beyond. Numerous courses both formal and do-it-yourself are available to help you achieve this.

2. You will need to train yourself to read 16th-century French specifically. Unfortunately I know of no specialist courses currently available in this, outside university courses in French literature that offer a 16th-century option. Basically, it is a matter of giving yourself lots of practice in reading 16th-century authors, preferably in the annotated paperback editions that various French publishers are so good at producing for their students. You would probably do best to start with the poet Ronsard, who is not too difficult and who is known to have admired Nostradamus's writings. Having mastered him, you should attempt to tackle at least the more straightforward chapters of Rabelais, who was actually at medical school with the future seer.

Q. How did 16th-century French differ from modern French, then?

A. Quite apart from the fact that it used relatively few accents and many of its spellings were different (not least because the idea of 'correct spelling' hadn't yet been invented), it had at its disposal a range of words that are now no longer used, as well as using familiar words in what to us are unfamiliar ways and expressing familiar ideas with quite different words. In addition, the fashion at the time was to import large numbers of Latin and Greek words, as well as dredging up and adapting old words from the past, strange words from regional dialects, specialist words from a range of obscure activities and even entirely invented words – as you can see happening in English, too, in the only slightly later plays of Shakespeare. And as if that were not enough, the subject-pronoun ('I', 'he', 'she', 'they') was often omitted, the negative signalled by a simple *ne* and the word-order freely modelled on Latin (so that the past participle, for example, was often shovelled to the end of its clause, as it still is in German).

3. You should then move on to the easier writings of Nostradamus himself. You might have a shot at his 'cookbook', the *Traité des fardemens et confitures*, especially as an (unfortunately corrupt and unreliable) English 'crib' is also available under the title *The Elixirs of Nostradamus* (Bloomsbury). The French original is quite straightforward, much friendlier than Mrs Beeton, and actually available in facsimile. Next on your list might be any extracts from his *Almanachs* that you can get hold of (their whereabouts are listed in the *Nostradamus Encyclopedia*). Graduating to his poetry, you could try your hand at reading his work on Egyptian hieroglyphs, the *Orus Apollo*

– though you should not take what he says too seriously. And finally you should tackle his easier prophecies in the *Sixains* before proceeding first to the *Présages*, then to the *Centuries* themselves, and lastly to the extremely obtuse *Préface à César* and *Lettre à Henri II* that go with them. Details of these and how to obtain them will be found in the list below or in Further Reading.

4. You will need adequate French dictionaries. At the very least you will need the largest possible modern French–English dictionary – or, better still, something even larger such as the French–English section of the two-volume work by J.E. Mansion first published by Harrap in 1934. Dictionaries not having yet been invented in Nostradamus's time, you will also need a good French etymological dictionary, so that you can trace the earlier forms of modern French words along with their former meanings. A good English dictionary showing derivations, such as *Chambers 20th Century Dictionary*, can also help – provided you bear in mind that it was never designed to reveal deep truths about French!

5. You will need access to good classical dictionaries, too. While a Greek dictionary can help occasionally, a large Latin dictionary is absolutely essential. This should be as old as possible, since older compilations included the all-important mythological and geographical information that modern ones often do not.

6. Nostradamus's prophecies being tied so closely to place-names (some of them little known), you will need not merely a general atlas but good detailed road atlases of Europe in general and France in particular. A good multi-

volume encyclopaedia or reference guide to the ancient world – once again, the older the better – will also help you to identify the names by which some modern places were once known and by which Nostradamus was (in keeping with his classically minded times) understandably keen to refer to them.

7. In order to work out the seer's astrological datings you will need good planetary ephemerides. For the years 1900 to 2050 these are readily available in printed form. But for dates further afield you will need a computerised ephemeris, such as you will find advertised in good astrology magazines.

8. Finally, of course, you will need to find copies of the original French editions. Reprints of the earliest available version of *Centuries* VIII to X are fairly readily available in a variety of publications. But only one book currently available in English contains *Centuries* I to VII, together with the *Sixains*, in their original editions (see the list below), and only two contain the original version of all the *Présages*.

Q. What are the original editions, and where can I find them?

A. The main editions of the *Propheties* are as follows:

The 1555 edition, covering *Centuries* I.1 to IV.53 only, plus the *Préface à César*. Michel Chomarat's 1984 facsimile of this is unfortunately no longer in print, but a transliteration of it is to be found in the *Nostradamus Encyclopedia* (see list below and Further Reading).

The much more roughly printed 1557 edition,

probably revised by Nostradamus himself, which covers *Centuries* I.1 to VII.40 (minus VI.100) and the *Préface à César*. Michel Chomarat's 1993 facsimile of this is available at the time of writing from the Maison de Nostradamus (for address see p. 119). Verses IV.54 to VII.40 of it are also transliterated in the *Nostradamus Encyclopedia*.

The posthumous, omnibus 1568 edition, which contains *Centuries* I.1 to VII.42 and VIII.1 to X.100, plus the *Préface à César* and the *Lettre à Henri II*. Of these, the *Centuries* are reprinted by Cheetham and Hogue, and the *Préface* and *Lettre* by Hogue only (see list below). The *Nostradamus Encyclopedia* reprints all except *Centuries* I.1 to VII.40, which are already covered by its transliterations of the earlier editions.

The 1605 edition. This contains everything in the previous paragraph, but in a slightly corrupt version. Also included are the 'extra quatrains', the *Présages* and the *Sixains*. Of these, only the *Présages* and 'extra quatrains' are reprinted by Hogue. The *Nostradamus Encyclopedia* reprints both these and the *Sixains*.

The 1672 edition by Théophile de Garencières. This edition, used by Roberts (see list below), is similar to that of 1568, but so very corrupt as to be worth steering well clear of.

On top of all this, of course, you will need lots of time and application – and even then you will be duplicating a great deal of work that has already been done. At this point you may well think it worth considering the alternative option.

Q. Before going on to the alternative, isn't there some simpler way of getting to grips with the French itself?

After all, I'm pretty intuitive, and I often find that by taking what I know of Latin, plus my couple of years of school French and odd snippets of Spanish and Italian, I can meditate on a verse and manage a fair stab at what it means ...

A. Unfortunately a 'fair stab' is the best that this approach is likely to achieve – even if it doesn't actually prove fatal. Nostradamus went to great pains to write his prophecies in rhyming verse, using a whole range of sophisticated linguistic techniques to say exactly what he wanted to say. If *you* want to discover exactly what he wanted to say, therefore, you are going to have to pay careful attention to the way in which he wrote it. Vaguely meditating on the verse is no way of achieving this, any more than vaguely meditating on the weather forecast is likely to reveal to you whether or when to take an umbrella ...

Plan B – Use Somebody Else's Research

There are dangers, of course, in relying too much on other people's research. For a start, you can never be sure how sound it is, especially if you yourself are approaching the subject as a newcomer. All the way from the texts themselves, via the necessary historical, geographical and etymological research, to the translations and the particular spin that they choose to put on them, you are totally in the hands of other people who, for all you know, may be completely unqualified for the job. They may know little history or geography. They may know even less French. In attempting their translations they may possibly have relied almost exclusively on heavy-footed, word-for-word dictionary work that is, of all approaches, the least designed to reveal a text's true meaning. They may well never have been trained in translation, or even have the first idea of what translation from language to language actually involves.

Certainly there is scarcely one of the published translations of Nostradamus that would be accepted in literary circles for a minute were it of Ronsard or Rabelais, say. No wonder Nostradamus is commonly regarded in the English-speaking world as some kind of illiterate!

Q. Doesn't the fact that such translations are published mean that they are OK? Surely somebody vets this kind of thing?

A. No, unfortunately nobody does. The publishers are for the most part just as much in the dark as most of their readers, and the experts are far too thin on the ground. The fact that something is in print, consequently, is no guarantee whatever of its accuracy or validity. The idea that it does constitute such a guarantee possibly goes back to the fact that one of the first books printed in Europe was the Bible – rather than the *Beano*, say.

What should you do, then? Accept *my* word for it? Surely not – since, for all you know, I am as ignorant as all the rest, notwithstanding my claim to be a university-trained linguist, as well as a former senior modern languages teacher and professional translator.

The answer lies in a more canny, *comparative* approach. Following is a survey of all the main translations and commentaries currently available in English. Most of them offer word-for-word versions of the most clumsy and unrepresentative kind, and often are grammatically and syntactically inaccurate into the bargain. Yet translations of this kind do have one advantage: you can actually see what each word theoretically means, provided that the author has done his or her dictionary work properly.

Q. How many of the authors *have* done their dictionary work properly?

A. Not many, in point of fact. Carelessness, vagueness and inaccuracy are common, and unwarranted linguistic conclusions are continually jumped to. Nevertheless, at least the word-equivalents will in the majority of cases be the nearest possible ones – always bearing in mind that French words don't really mean English words anyway.

Taking one of the better examples of the 'literal' approach, then, you can now compare it with a much freer, more idiomatic version – one that attempts to render the seer's verses into similarly styled English verse. This latter, if it is any good, will at least have the advantage of conveying the same general meaning and impression as the original text, rather than treating it as if it were some kind of legal document. It will be a true *translation*, in other words.

Unfortunately, though, there is only one known major verse-translation of this type to date (see below), and it suffers from the inevitable drawbacks of this kind of approach (there is *no* way of translating Nostradamus, alas, that doesn't have its drawbacks!). Although much more readable and understandable than the word-for-word versions, it is inevitably fairly free, too, and occasionally, like any verse-translation, has to resort to 'padding' and compression in order to a) fit the space available and b) rhyme.

However, your exercise in comparison will quickly show up these 'introduced' bits for what they are, and enable you to arrive at a fair assessment of just how far the more representative 'literary' version actually fits the original individual words.

This will not solve all your problems of interpretation and dating, of course. Here you will need a good general book on Nostradamus that will place him in his true cultural and historical context, as well as throwing some light on his methods and the historical and geographical facts on which they are based (see the titles discussed below and the Further Reading section). A good planetary ephemeris, too, will help you decode the various astrological references.

In this way you will effectively bypass the oddities and incompetencies of any individual author, and hopefully be able to arrive at an objective assessment of what the prophecies are saying. However, you will still need to arrange the verses in their proper sequence if you are to establish the true context within which each individual prophecy is meant to be understood – and there are (as you will see below) only three or four books which even attempt to establish such a sequence.

Available Translations and Interpretations

Slash marks indicate UK/US publications.

Erika Cheetham's *The Prophecies of Nostradamus* (Spearman, 1973, Corgi, 1975/Perigree, 1991) consists of the *Centuries* only, in a fairly reliable transcription of the 1568 edition. It is an excellent source for the French text, but the translations are unfortunately not so trustworthy. The author herself admits that they are relatively crude and literal, but they are also full of quite basic errors. Although her research has been extensive, again it is not reliable, especially in terms of biography and etymology. Her interpretations are often somewhat 'stretched' and credulous, but she is honest enough to admit that there are many quatrains that she cannot interpret.

The same author's *The Final Prophecies of Nostradamus* (Futura/Perigree, 1989) once again consists of the *Centuries* alone, also in the 1568 edition, but this time even more exactly transcribed; this makes it a good French source for students of Nostradamus. The same drawbacks as before apply, though – the translations are literal and not always reliable, and although some earlier errors have been corrected others have crept in. The interpretations have been updated, but more in the light of recent events than of further research into Nostradamus.

Herbert G.B. Erickstad's *The Prophecies of Nostradamus in Historical Order* (Janus, 1996/Vantage, 1982) contains some 350 of the verses, arranged in proposed sequence. The source is not specified but seems to be the 1568 edition. The literal translations are accompanied by generally out-of-date research apparently based on Cheetham. However, the research does contain some useful insights based on the author's own travels to many of the places pinpointed. Erickstad's interpretations for the past rely mostly on Cheetham, but those for the future make use of the author's own sequencing, which produces some remarkably objective and reasonable results. This book is an interesting attempt to approach the question of meaning scientifically and without too much subjective input. An important drawback is that it is difficult to track down given quatrains since there is no index.

Jean-Charles de Fontbrune's *Nostradamus I: Countdown to Apocalypse* (Pan/Holt, 1983; Cresset, 1993, Part 1) consists of the first of some 600 selected verses from the *Centuries*, *Présages* and *Sixains*, placed in attempted sequence and taken exclusively from the already corrupt 1605 edition. The English translations (from Fontbrune's original modern French versions) are more in the nature of interpretations. The interpretations themselves are at times tendentious, but Fontbrune's attempt at sequencing is certainly admirable. His extensive and laborious research mainly comprises lengthy translated quotations from French textbooks. Although this is a widely read version it cannot be recommended as a good source for either texts or translations, and is not well regarded by French Nostradamus scholars.

Fontbrune's *Nostradamus 2: Into the Twenty-First Century* (Holt, 1984; Cresset, 1993, Part 2) is a translation from the French *Nostradamus, historien et prophète*, Vol. 2 (Editions du Rocher, 1980) and consists of a further sequenced selection, as above. Most of the same remarks apply. Designed to deal with the residue of verses sequenced by Fontbrune and his eminent father, this volume alone contains the all-important index to both books.

For beautiful books on Nostradamus you could go for John Hogue – but, sadly, not for serious study. His *Nostradamus and the Millennium* (Bloomsbury, 1987) contains no original texts but only a few highly selected and heavily interpreted word-for-word translations. As regards Nostradamus, the research is flawed and out of date. The illustrations include two pages of alleged Nostradamus manuscript that unfortunately bear no resemblance to his writing. Hogue's interpretations are somewhat tendentious and dedicated to a particular view of the immediate future featuring some of his own favourite saints and villains, backed up by unconvincing, selected attempts to link verse-numbers with dates.

The same author's magnificently produced and illustrated *Nostradamus: The New Revelations* (Element/Element 1994) again contains none of Nostradamus's own texts. Its six hundred or so literally translated verses are arbitrarily selected (and sometimes just as arbitrarily dismembered). The limited research is extremely out of date, and the interpretations are as tendentious as before and based on premises that are just as questionable. The piece of bogus Nostradamus manuscript once again makes its appearance, and the picture of 'St Remy de Provence, the birthplace of Nostradamus' on the title page, which begs to be taken as that of his house, shows the right street (if local tradition is to be believed) but the wrong building.

Still with Hogue, his *Nostradamus: The Complete Prophecies* (Element/Element 1997) contains the *Centuries*, *Préface* and *Lettre à Henri II*, directly transcribed from the 1568 edition, plus the *Présages* and 'extra quatrains' from the 1605 edition (further edited by Hogue), but not including the *Sixains*. This magnificently comprehensive and dense treatment of nearly a thousand pages without a single illustration includes some good reference sections too. But there, unfortunately, the plaudits have to stop. Although the translations are more careful than before, they are still both literalistic and heavily interpreted (an apparent paradox which helps to demonstrate just how unreliable literal translation can be!). The research is more extensive than previously, but as far as Nostradamus himself is concerned still out of touch. Once again Hogue's interpretations are fairly subjective (as he himself admits) and thus heavily skewed towards his own personal themes for the future, including his familiar cast of favourite terrorists and gurus.

Of my own two interpretational books on the seer,

Nostradamus – The Next 50 Years (Piatkus, 1993/Berkley, 1994) contains the only sequenced English verse translation to date of some 430 of the prophecies, based on the 1568 edition and indexed to permit easy reference to individual prophecies. I have made no attempt to be literally exact, preferring to aim at giving an impression of the sense and style of the original verses (none of which is included). The research, based originally on Cheetham, has been updated in later editions. My interpretations are based heavily on sequencing, which hopefully makes them less subjective than usual. For study purposes, this kind of relatively free translation could usefully be compared with a more literal version, such as Edgar Leoni's *Nostradamus and His Prophecies* – and notes are provided to assist readers who wish to do so.

My *Nostradamus: The Final Reckoning* (Piatkus, 1995/Berkley, 1997) once again includes no original Nostradamus texts, but does contain a number of new verse translations (not indexed) including 27 of the *Sixains*. New research offers fresh insights into Nostradamus's 'liturgical count', plus comparisons with other prophets. The intention, as before, is to avoid personal preconceptions, so the interpretations are, once again, based mainly on sequencing. Over 150 actual dates are suggested in the course of a 'calendar of the future', accompanied by campaign maps for what is claimed to be a coming Islamic invasion of Europe.

My *Nostradamus Encyclopedia* (Godsfield, 1997/St Martin's, 1997) is, as the title suggests, an all-embracing treatment of the prophet and his works. It contains texts of all the prophecies transliterated from the earliest available French editions (1555, 1557, 1568 and 1605) and is the only UK/US source published to date for the English language market that contains the texts of the original 1555 and 1557 editions. Although there are few actual translations, all the prophecies are accompanied by factual English paraphrases. The research is the most comprehensive and up-to-date available in English at present. Profusely annotated and indexed, with a gazetteer and specialist Nostradamus dictionary, this work is a useful one for readers wishing to consult the original texts, but not, clearly, for those looking for translations.

Edgar Leoni's *Nostradamus and His Prophecies* (Wings, 1961–82) contains a magnificent collection of original texts: all the *Centuries*, the *Présages*, the *Preface à César*, the *Lettre à Henri II*, the 'extra quatrains', the letters to Jean Morel and the canons of Orange – even the false prophecies of Orval and Olivarius. The main texts are based on late copies of the 1555 and 1568 editions and the original 1605 version – though with spellings modernised by Leoni! His very literal translations unfortunately tend to ignore the complexities of the original syntax. The research, extensive at the time of publication, is now rather dated. Leoni's interpretations are encouragingly undogmatic and wide-ranging, though obviously limited to the research available at the time of writing.

The only currently available facsimile of an original edition of Nostradamus's prophecies is *Les Propheties: Lyon 1557*. This was published by Editions Michel Chomarat in 1993 and can be obtained from the Maison de Nostradamus in Salon (for address see p.119). It consists of the 1557 edition (verses I.1 to VII.40, minus VI.100, with the earlier verses possibly revised from the original 1555 edition by the prophet himself.

Back among the interpretations again, Stefan Paulus's *Nostradamus 2000: Who Will Survive?* (O'Hara, 1997/ Llewellyn 1996) contains some extremely interesting information on Muslim and other apocalyptic beliefs, but cannot really be recommended otherwise. The highly selective

French text is from an unspecified, but apparently very late, edition, and is complemented by over-literal and often ill-informed translations. There is little or no research regarding the texts, and the interpretations are skewed to revolve around the author's own decidedly oddball understanding of verse X.72.

Finally, Henry C. Roberts's *The Complete Prophecies of Nostradamus* (Grafton/Nostradamus Co., 1985) is rather less complete than the title claims. It consists merely of the *Centuries*, the *Préface*, the *Lettre à Henri II* and the 'extra quatrains', all based on Garencières' extremely corrupt 1672 edition. The translations are literal, but sometimes offer useful insights. In its time (the book was first published in 1947) Roberts's work was original and pioneering, but it has long since fallen by the wayside in the light of later books. His interpretations are brief, but often rather wild in terms of geography and history, and the book's only real usefulness is as a source of comparison with other editions.

For more titles, see Chapter 10 and Further Reading, which follows it.

7

How Did He Do It?
(1)

Comparative Horoscopy

To judge by most would-be biographies of him, you would think that Nostradamus was some kind of godlike (or possibly demonic) super-being who wielded awesome magical powers of foresight. Indeed, he himself was not above encouraging that impression. In fact, however, as the more canny of his contemporaries were well aware, he was just an ordinary, rather confused doctor and academic who had had the luck to stumble on some striking mathematical and meditative techniques at just the right time, and used the fact both to foretell the future history of the world and to make his own name.

As Arthur C. Clarke's Third Law so perceptively puts it, 'Any sufficiently advanced technology is indistinguishable from magic.'

Ever since about 1540 interest had been growing in astronomy and astrology, and particularly in the cycles (or 'revolutions') of the planets – a term which, at the time, included the sun and moon. As a result, a whole series of astrologers had published books on the subject, from Petrus Apianus (1540) to Scaliger's former mentor Luca Gaurico (1545), by way of Cardano, Mussemius, Postel, Leowitz, Turrel and Roussat – the last three of them all known to have been referred to by Nostradamus.

To say nothing, of course, of the great Nicolaus Copernicus, whose *On the Revolutions of the Celestial Orbs* appeared in 1543.

Q. Is it true that Nostradamus had the 'Copernican' idea that the planets revolve around the sun even before Copernicus?

A. There is no actual evidence for this, though it would be surprising if the idea had not been at least 'in the air' at the time – or Copernicus himself might never have researched it. The Polish-German astronomer, after all, had been working on the theory since at least 1505, and sharing his ideas with his closest associates.

Many of these books contained detailed tables for calculating the monthly positions of the planets not only for centuries to come, but far into the past, too. Apianus had even supplied with his book a kind of cardboard computer – rather like that once used by pilots to navigate on their knees – whose adjustable discs allowed users to calculate the sign in which any given planet would find itself in any given month.

There was no attempt to be too precise about it, of course. Calculating exact aspects in terms of degrees and minutes was not to be expected of calculations extending so far into the past and future. But working out *in which signs* the planets would be during any given month was perfectly possible, given that each sign covered a twelfth of the heavens – which meant, of course, that is was also possible to calculate when two or more of them would be in the same sign at once. This supposedly highly significant event was referred to as a 'conjunction', which was thus a rather wider concept than modern astrologers generally attach to the term.

And it boded no end of unspecified evil and disaster.

Q. Are you saying that the astronomers and astrologers of Nostradamus's day actually had telescopes good enough to predict conjunctions and other planetary configurations centuries ahead of time?

A. No, they didn't have the telescope at all. It wasn't invented (officially, at least) until 1608, over 40 years after Nostradamus's death. But you don't need a telescope to calculate where the planets will be relative to the position of the sun at the spring equinox – which is what putting them in their correct 'signs' amounts to. People had had perfectly efficient astrolabes and other instruments for doing that for centuries past.

Indeed, if you doubt their ability to do so, remember that both Turrel and Roussat managed (the latter in 1550) to calculate the major planetary line-up of 1789 (over 200 years ahead), and interpreted it as signifying some huge social upheaval.

An upheaval which, as we now know, turned out to be the French Revolution.

It may have been a major conjunction that occurred in 1524, during Nostradamus's days as a young apothecary, that first gave him the idea of how such phenomena might be used to predict the future. For that same conjunction had occurred before, in 1186, albeit in a different sign. Sun, Mercury, Venus, Mars, Jupiter and Saturn – all the then-known planets except the moon – had aligned themselves in Libra, just as in his own day they were about to do in Pisces. This meant, incidentally, that (under the primitive 'Babylonian' system of astrological 'houses' that Nostradamus then preferred) they would all on both occasions have been in the tenth house at approximately 11 o'clock in the morning.

What awful events, then, might the coming line-up portend?

Nostradamus's blinding insight seems, like most blinding insights, to have been an extraordinarily simple one – that you could actually look back to the last time it had happened in order to find out.

So what *had* happened in 1186?

So far as anybody could tell from the history books, nothing of any importance at all, at least in France and western Europe.

So perhaps this meant that nothing would happen this time, either?

In the event, certainly, nothing did. This fact may well have confirmed the young apothecary in the novel idea that direct reference to past astrological patterns could be used to predict the future. The idea fitted in perfectly with current ideas on human knowledge. It was absolutely axiomatic to contemporary thought, as we have seen, that all the answers lay in the past. What more natural, then, than that the keys to humanity's astrologically determined future should lie in the past, too?

Q. Does this mean that nothing special will happen in May 2000, either, when the same planets line up in Taurus?

A. Perhaps. But in May 2000 there is a difference, in that the moon will join in as well. This could just possibly be astrologically significant.

This was the basic idea that the later seer was to grab with both hands. By looking at where the planets were the last time something important happened you could actually work out when it would happen next, simply by calculating when the same planets would return to the same signs again.

It was, I repeat, an absurdly simple idea and so, when Nostradamus finally mentioned the fact publicly, in his open letter to his son on completion of part one of the *Propheties*, he was understandably careful to make it look as complicated as possible. The most that he was prepared to say was that the 'astronomical revolutions' that were constantly 'meshing in with past, present and future developments' could be used to calculate the 'latitudinary dimension at which God will complete the circuit where the celestial images will return to exert themselves'.

'Nothing could be clearer,' I was going to say, but then for Nostradamus, clarity was always a relative matter ...

On this matter of calculation the seer was always most insistent – especially throughout his subsequent covering letter to the King. He had, he said, 'reckoned and calculated the present prophecies entirely according to the order of the chain which encompasses its circuit'. The verbal obfuscation was deliberate, but underneath it you can detect readily enough the idea that repetitions of planetary configurations lay at the heart of his whole approach. That the predictions had also benefited from other, more occult techniques he also admitted – but more on these in Chapter 8.

How, then, did this primary technique of comparative horoscopy work in practice?

Nostradamus's first step was necessarily to select a range of outstanding historical events, mainly from classical times, but not excluding more dramatic recent events. Possibly, there was no particular method in this. He simply went for the events which most readily sprang to mind.

If so, there was an almost inevitable corollary. If you try doing the same yourself, you will almost certainly find that at least 90 per cent of the events you have selected are disasters of various kinds. 'Good' events are often less easily pinpointed, slower to develop and consequently less striking to the eye. To that extent, then, it is not too surprising that doom and disaster are the things that most readily spring out from Nostradamus's pages.

Having established a range of events, he now had to establish just where the various planets were at the time. Or rather, *not* at the time. Experiential evidence suggests that he in fact took the planets as they were during the run-up to each event, rather than at the time of the event itself.

Quite why this should be is open to question. Possibly either his tables or his reading of them were in error. Possibly he was trying to apply a 'Gregorian' correction even before our modern Gregorian calendar was invented, but – not uncharacteristically, perhaps – in the wrong direction. (There were ten days' difference between the two in his day, and the new, Gregorian version would not come into effect until 1582.) But it is perhaps more likely that, in deference to the theory that the positions of the planets relate to the *causes* of events and the influences surrounding them, rather than to the events themselves, he was attempting to pinpoint their *dates of causation*. This might tie in with the fact that, by and large, small, sudden events seem to be pinpointed by short, quite recent planetary configurations, whereas longer and larger events seem to relate to earlier and longer-term celestial patterns.

This does not apply merely to Nostradamus, incidentally. My own independent research tends to suggest this, too, insofar as the idea of comparative horoscopy can be considered valid in the first place.

Q. But *is* comparative horoscopy valid? Are events in the heavens really linked to events on earth in the way that you are suggesting Nostradamus believed?

A. That's the big question. By Einsteinian definition, whatever happens anywhere in the universe affects the rest of it, too. On the other hand, it is virtually impossible to detect or measure planetary influences scientifically. Indeed, perhaps it is not a matter of 'influences' at all, but of the planets reflecting what is happening to the universe as a whole at any one time, just as events on earth do, too.

As the ancient Hermetic formula put it, 'As Above, so Below'.

Perhaps the best that can be done is to examine the evidence presented on the topic here and in my *Nostradamus Encyclopedia*. If the historical links appear to be substantiated more often than chance would suggest, they are presumably real. At which point, clearly, somebody has some explaining to do ...

How, then, would Nostradamus have found out where the various planets were in ancient times? There were plenty of Greek and Roman horoscopes still available for major events of the past. The Romans particularly were intensely superstitious, and were reluctant to undertake anything important without the sanction either of the stars or of the various oracles, and particularly of the Sibylline oracle at Cumae, near Naples. Even where such horoscopes were lacking, however, the seer now had a whole panoply of astronomical tables available – to say nothing of Apianus's cardboard computer.

So he would have had little difficulty, for example, in discovering the positions of the planets at the time of the assassination of Julius Caesar in 44 BC, or of the official accession of his successor, the Emperor Augustus, in 27 BC, or of the Spartacus slave revolt of 73–71 BC. And indeed, as I have shown in my *Nostradamus Encyclopedia*, the assassination of Caesar does show a remarkable planetary match with the assassination of President J.F. Kennedy in 1963 (if, indeed, Nostradamus predicted it at all – which is by no means certain). Similarly, the accession of Augustus and the subsequent period of peace and prosperity that is clearly reflected in verse X.89 (since it virtually quotes Augustus's own words about having found a Rome built of brick and left one built of marble), does seem to predict – via a five-planet match – a period of peace and post-war reconstruction starting in 1945.

Even though, admittedly, the seer mistakenly (if characteristically) counts the 57 years of Augustus's reign, clearly referred to in the verse, from what the planetary dating defines as Augustus's official enthronement, instead of (as he should have done) from his *unofficial* accession on the earlier death of Caesar . . .

But certainly such a period of peace and post-war reconstruction did begin in Europe in 1945 – the only difference being that the material in which Europe's city centres were being rebuilt at the time was not white marble but white concrete. The only question, therefore, is whether that period will really last until 2002.

What, then, of the Spartacus slave revolt? Here there are

in fact two matches, one of four planets and the other of five, the latter of which he was specifically to refer to in his covering letter to the King.

Q. Why was he satisfied with mere four- or five-planet matches? Shouldn't he have been looking for matches of *all* the planets?

A. It would have been nice. Unfortunately, though, the chances against *all* the planets ever reappearing at once in exactly the same signs as before are almost infinite. If the astrological indications in his quatrains are to be believed, Nostradamus sometimes seems to have been satisfied with matches of as few as three planets, provided that they were sufficiently far out, and the matches therefore unusual enough. But, clearly, matches of four, five or six planets are much more satisfactory. These last, though, are very rare – especially bearing in mind that, including the sun and moon, only seven planets (as far out as Saturn) were known in Nostradamus's day.

It was the year 71 BC that saw the final stages of the Spartacus slave revolt. The ephemeris, or planetary table, for 25–27 May that year shows the sun in Gemini, the moon passing from Virgo (where Mars also was) to Libra (where Jupiter also was), and Mercury in Taurus. Whether the actual dates were significant or not (and one gets the impression that, where very ancient events were concerned, Nostradamus was often satisfied merely to get the right *year*), this same pattern would, as it happened, be repeated between 20 May and 6 June 1792.

By way of illustrating such matches, I like to depict both

HOROGRAPH FOR: 25 May 71 BC TO: 27 May 71 BC

	Aries	Tauru	Gemin	Cance	Leo	Virgo	Libra	Scorp	Sagit	Capri	Aquar	Pisce
Pluto		✶										
Neptune			✶									
Uranus		✶										
Saturn										✶		
Jupiter							★					
Mars						★						
Venus			✶									
Mercury		★										
Moon						★	★					
Sun			★									

Solar noon declination (to nearest degree): 21°N

Geographical latitude: 46°N to 38°N

LOCATION: Italy

EVENT: Roman slave revolt under Spartacus (final stages)

situations in the form of a pair of what I call 'horographs' — simplified horoscopic charts that dispense with all the mumbo-jumbo of the conventional horoscope (since this is superfluous to the task in hand), and that instead show only which planets are in which signs:

HOROGRAPH FOR: 20 May 1792   TO: 6 June 1792

	Aries	Tauru	Gemin	Cance	Leo	Virgo	Libra	Scorp	Sagit	Capri	Aquar	Pisce
Pluto											☆	
Neptune							☆					
Uranus												
Saturn	☆											
Jupiter							★					
Mars						★						
Venus		☆										
Mercury		★										
Moon		☆		☆	☆	★	★	☆	☆	☆		
Sun			★									

Solar noon declination (to nearest degree):   20°N to 23°N

Relative latitude: 1°S to 2°N   Geographical latitude: 48°N to 37°N (±1°)

POSSIBLE LOCATION: Orléans, France, southwards to Corsica, Sardinia and southern Italy

EVENT: Closing stages of French Revolution and possible spread to Italy

Here it can readily be seen how the planets that I have just listed (here shown in solid black) were all in precisely the same signs on both occasions, so fixing the 'dates of causation' of the later event, too. Moreover, on the basis of the sun's changing declination throughout the year, it is (and was) possible to adjust the latitude of the original event to determine that of the later one – and it turns out to be that of Orléans southwards, though possibly (in the light of the proposed tolerance of 1° either way) as far north as Paris, at nearly 49° north.

Q. How about the longitude? How did Nostradamus actually fix the future places involved?

A. It wasn't possible to calculate longitude in Nostradamus's day because accurate chronometers hadn't yet been invented. But two possible approaches were available to him. First, he could rely on the arbitrary allocation of countries, regions and cities to astrological signs. France and northern Italy, for example, were assigned to Aries, to say nothing of England, Belgium, Holland, Germany, Palestine, Syria, Poland and Sweden. Anything that originally happened in an 'Arian' country (so Nostradamus seems to have assumed – when it suited him, at least) must happen in an 'Arian' country in the future too. But since this was far too blunt an instrument for events within Europe, his second option was to rely on the fact that capital cities must be reflected in capital cities, ports in ports, mountains in mountains, islands in islands and so on. Theoretically, in other words, all he had to do was follow the new latitude band (and Nostradamus mentions latitudes frequently, often via the word *climat*, from the Greek *klima*, which refers to the altitude of the sun) until it encountered a feature of just the type required. Study of the *Propheties* shows that the place-names in individual verses often follow just the kind of clearly defined latitude bands that this method tends to throw up.

In view of this, it is no surprise to find the seer referring in his letter to the King *not* to 1789 – the year pinpointed by most others on the basis merely of that year's major planetary conjunction – but to 'the year one thousand seven hundred and ninety-two, which will be thought to be (the beginning of) a new age'. And so indeed it turned out to be, with the eventual proclamation at the end of September (well after the horoscopic date, in line with the magnitude of the event) of the French Republic. As for the fact that 71 BC marked the final *failure* of the Spartacus revolt, while 1792 marked the final *success* of the French Revolution, the difference might be accounted for by the fact that Saturn, formerly in its own sign of Capricorn, was now in Aries (here, though, we are more in the realms of traditional astrology, with all its scope for individual interpretation). Alternatively it could be argued that September 1792 marked not the *success* of the French Revolution, but its ultimate *betrayal*, leading as it did to foreign war, beheadings and a Reign of Terror that culminated not in the hoped-for democracy and freedom, but in the ultimate despotism of Napoleon Bonaparte.

But Nostradamus seems to have foreseen some of this, too. 'Afterwards,' he went on, 'the Roman people will pick themselves up again and chase away various dark shadows while receiving (i.e. recovering?) some measure of their original light, not without great division and continual upheavals.' Though quite whom he really meant by the 'Roman people' is anybody's guess. Could this, perhaps, be yet another sign of the apparent 'Italian' component in the second horograph?

This particular planetary match I have already demonstrated in my *Nostradamus Encyclopedia*. For the purposes of the current book, however, I felt that I should search out a previously unpublished major match. It occurred to me that a suitable base-event might be the one referred to by a group of at least five quatrains that are evidently devoted to a major counter-attack on the Middle East in the wake of a huge future Muslim invasion of Europe.

The five quatrains in question are II.22, I.74, VI.85, II.79 and VI.70, and they read, in my published translations (here slightly edited):

> Seaward from Europe sails th' amazing force:
> The Northern fleet its battle-line deploys.
> Near isle submerged it sets a common course.
> The great world's centre yields to stronger voice.

> Rested, on Epirus they'll set their sights.
> Deliverance next to Antioch they'll bring.
> The king with black, curled beard for th' Empire fights.
> Roasted shall be the copper-bearded king.

> By forces French shall mighty Tarsus be
> Destroyed, all Muslims captured, led away —
> Helped by the mighty Portuguese at sea —
> When summer starts, on good St Urban's day.

> By skill he of the curly beard and black
> The race both cruel and proud soon subjugates.
> Chyren the Great from far away brings back
> All those still penned by Muslim prison-gates.

> Head of the world great Chyren is acclaimed,
> 'Further Beyond' thereafter feared, adored.
> Well-pleased the only victor to be named,
> Heaven-high his fame and praise shall soon have soared.

Now there can be no doubt at all that these five verses are based on the Holy Roman Emperor Charles V's celebrated raid on Tunis of June 1535. In the course of it the city was captured, thousands of Christian prisoners were released from the prisons of the notorious Turkish vassal, the pirate Barbarossa II (i.e. 'Red Beard'), and his pirate fleet was destroyed. As a result, Charles was hailed throughout Europe as a mighty hero and the saviour of the hour.

The clues stand out a mile. The final verse's *plus oultre* is a version of the Latin *Plus Ultra* – in modern terms, something like 'Above and Beyond' – which was part of the motto of Charles V. I am not privy to the exact state of the Hapsburg Emperor's beard (certainly it was dark), but his opponent in the second verse quoted above is specifically described as *Barbe d'aerain*, or 'Bronze-beard' – an obvious Nostradamian transcription of 'Barbarossa'. It would follow that *Chyren* (a mysterious name that has been identified by virtually everybody from the seer's own secretary onwards as an anagram of 'Henryc', and thus as referring to the expected future saviour of France, the long-awaited Henri V) is destined to be a virtual reincarnation of the former Holy Roman Emperor.

True, the exact role of the Portuguese in all this is unclear, but several of the place-names are quite specific – the former Epirus in western Greece, Antioch (now Antakya) and Tarsus in southern Turkey – while the 'isle submerged' begs to be identified as the volcanic island of Santorini. Even a specific date is included – namely St Urban's Day, which is 25 May (as, of course, Nostradamus's own *Almanachs* reveal).

All this positively begs, then, for the identification of some future occasion when, thanks to comparative horoscopy, Charles's raid on Tunis is theoretically due to be repeated, but further to the east.

I therefore started looking for it in the normal way. I

printed out the ephemeris charts for May and June 1535 on the Julian calendar that was in force at the time. I then started searching for the expected future match. Not bothering to open the earlier book in which I had sequenced this whole complex of verses on the basis of other dating hints, I seemed vaguely to remember that I had originally dated the repetition to around 2034. I therefore called up the Gregorian ephemeris charts for May and June of that year.

Not a birdie!

This was unusual. Generally speaking, I have found that, when searching for future matches of a major historical event, it has been necessary only to identify which of Nostradamus's prophecies best matches it, and then to look up the year for which I have already sequenced it. In most cases all the relevant planets have been there, all lined up and waiting.

Q. Doesn't this just prove that you can find such planetary matches virtually anywhere? Can't you make almost any date fit?

A. No. If you have no idea of the year in question it can take an age to find the future match, as you will see from the rest of the story ...

On this occasion, though, there was no sign of a match. Curious, I wondered whether I had been 'retarding' events a little, and so looked up 2033.

Again, not a birdie.

Increasingly concerned, I looked up 2035 instead. Things were no more promising. Surely, I thought, it can't be as late as 2036? Almost in desperation, I called up the charts for May and June of that year in turn ...

And there the match was.

And *what* a match! No fewer than seven planets were lined up in their proper positions. The length of the time-window involved — and the consequent breadth of latitude band — suggested a major campaign rather than a mere raid. And there, within the period covered, was St Urban's Day (25 May) just as Nostradamus had predicted.

The relevant horographs are printed over the page, and so you can see for yourself just how extraordinary the match is. All the way out to Pluto the planets are virtually on parade, only waiting for us to pass them in review. This is the first time that this particular pattern has been repeated — and it will not occur again for several centuries.

Yet there are at least two oddities about this phenomenon. The first is that Nostradamus cannot possibly have realised all this, since for him it was merely a four-planet match (Uranus, Neptune and Pluto not yet having been discovered). And the second is that St Urban's Day actually falls *within* the astrological window, when theoretically (if my earlier analysis of the principles involved is right) it ought to fall well after it. This, of course, raises the question of whether the seer had some occult means of perceiving the match directly, perhaps through some form of clairvoyance.

This, indeed, is the question that we shall be considering in Chapter 8.

Incidentally, after making this discovery I did check back with the book to see when I actually *had* sequenced it for.

As you can see by referring back to p. 58, it was, after all, *for the period beginning in 2036 . . .*

HOROGRAPH FOR: 21 May 1535 **TO:** 24 May 1535

	Aries	Tauru	Gemin	Cance	Leo	Virgo	Libra	Scorp	Sagit	Capri	Aquar	Pisce
Pluto												
Neptune	★											
Uranus				★								
Saturn					★							
Jupiter												✷
Mars	✷											
Venus			★									
Mercury		★										
Moon											✷	✷
Sun			★									

Solar noon declination (to nearest degree): 22°N

Geographical latitude: 36° 47" N

LOCATION: Tunis, North Africa
EVENT: Victorious raid on pirate Barbarossa II by Emperor Charles V

HOROGRAPH FOR: 21 May 2036   TO: 11 June 2036

	Aries	Tauru	Gemin	Cance	Leo	Virgo	Libra	Scorp	Sagit	Capri	Aquar	Pisce
Pluto											★	
Neptune	★											
Uranus				★								
Saturn					★							
Jupiter			☼									
Mars				☼								
Venus			★									
Mercury		★										
Moon	☼	☼	☼	☼	☼	☼	☼	☼	☼	☼		
Sun			★									

Solar noon declination (to nearest degree):   20°N to 23°N

Relative latitude: 2°S to 1°N   Geographical latitude: 34°47'N to 37°47'N (±1°)

POSSIBLE LOCATION: From Bejaia, Tunis and Algiers, via the Cyclades, to Antakya and Tarsus

EVENT: Counter-invasion of Islamic Middle Eastern heartlands by Henri V of France

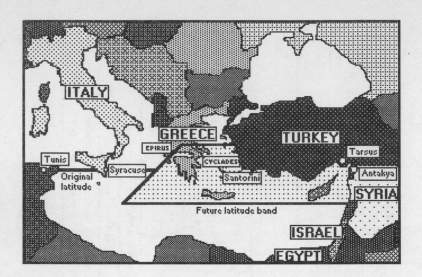

Henri V's reinvasion of the Middle East, 2036
The solar declination determines the future latitude band

8

How Did He Do It?
(2)

For all the evident clarity and accuracy of Nostradamus's technique of comparative horoscopy, it has a distinct feeling about it of potentiality rather than of actuality. To put it another way, the technique predicts not so much that an event *will* occur, as when and where it *might* occur. The potential is there, in other words, wherever the particular planetary match comes around again. But for the event actually to happen again, it still needs somebody to walk in and fulfil it.

What comparative horoscopy predicts, it seems, is merely a series of 'empty destinies' whose actual fulfilment or non-fulfilment still depends upon human choices.

Q. I thought Nostradamus's prophecies were supposed to be infallible?

A. Curiously enough, he does seem to suggest this in his covering letter to the King. '*Possum non errare, fall decepi*,' he writes in Latin, or 'It is possible for me n to err, fail or be deceived.' However, it is not clear that he really meant he could never be wrong. In his letter to the canons of Orange of 4 February 1562, after all, he states the opposite: '*Humanus sum, possum errare, falli, decepi*' or 'I am human: I can err, fail and be deceived.' Elsewhere in his royal letter, too, he does admit of the possibility of error, so it would seem that the infallibility of Nostradamus wasn't an article of faith, even for Nostradamus. Besides, he always allowed for 'acts of God': 'God', he constantly asserted in his *Almanachs*, is 'above the stars'.

This accent on mere potentiality could account for the fact that the seer occasionally gives alternative dates. *Sixain* 16, for example, suggests (via his 'liturgical count') a date of October/November 1997 *or* June/July 1998 for a British royal accession or a surprise American presidential inauguration (it is not entirely clear which).

In point of fact, though, neither happened in October/November 1997. And yet at that time there was a strong and hitherto unexpected feeling in the air (duly mirrored in the British media) that Queen Elizabeth II might shortly abdicate in the light of the monarchy's perceived out-of-touchness following the death of Diana, Princess of Wales, while the presidency of Bill Clinton was, not for the first time, teetering on the brink in the wake of allegations of sexual misconduct and (in this particular case) of consequent lying.

Since neither event actually happened at that particular juncture it still remains to be seen at the time of writing whether a similar climate will prevail in June/July 1998, and whether any concrete action will result.

By the time you read this, you will no doubt know the answer. That, at least, is a prediction that I feel safe in making!

In view of the fact that comparative horoscopy tended to give him only 'empty destinies', then, Nostradamus needed other sources of insight to tell him whether they would actually be fulfilled. And this is where his other, more occult techniques seem to have come into play.

Divination

Fortunately for us, Nostradamus describes in his very first two verses the main complementary prophetic techniques that he used. He constantly refers to them, too, in the *Préface* and Letter to Henri II.

In slightly edited versions of my previous published translations, the two verses in question read:

> *Seated, at ease, the secret eremite*
> *On brazen tripod studies through the night.*
> *What 'midst the lonely darkness flickers bright*
> *Bids fair to bring what none should doubt to light.*

> *Wand placed in hand as once in Branchis' fane,*
> *He dips in water both his hem and feet.*
> *A dread voice shakes him in his gown amain,*
> *Then light divine! The god assumes his seat.*

True, for 'fane' it would be better to read 'holy of holies': my slight transformation is, I am afraid, one of the almost inevitable consequences of verse-translation.

But then the original verses are themselves freely adapted verse-translations. Both of them are taken from the 3rd/ 4th-century neo-Platonist philosopher Iamblichus's *De Mysteriis Aegyptiorum*, itself a Latin translation of the original Greek, and republished in 1549 by a future publisher of

Nostradamus himself, Jean de Tournes, possibly at the former's behest. The first verse quoted is from Iamblichus's description of what used to happen at the Delphic oracle in ancient Greece,

> 'The prophetess at Delphi receives the god in two ways,' he writes, 'Whether through a subtle and fiery spirit that spurts up through the mouth of the cavern, or sitting in the inner shrine on a brazen tripod or a four-footed stool sacred to the divinity, she surrenders herself completely to the god, and is illuminated with a ray of divine fire. And once, indeed, the fiery mist arising from the aperture has surrounded her densely, she is filled by it with a divine splendour (Nostradamus's original terms exactly!). Moreover, when she takes the seat of the god, she merges herself with his unwavering prophetic power, and from these two preparatory procedures she becomes entirely the god's mouthpiece. As a result of which, suddenly the god is present, illuminating her in her own right, and quite separate from the fire, the spirit, their respective seats and all the visible apparatus of the place, whether man-made or sacred.'

and the second is based on Iamblichus's immediate sequel concerning the oracle at Branchidai:

> 'The prophetess at Branchidai (the De Tournes version actually has 'Brancis', but still refers to the former oracle of Apollo at what is now Didymi in Turkey), whether she holds in her hand a wand, originally presented by some god, and becomes filled with divine splendour, or whether she sits on a wheel and foretells future events, or dips her feet or the hem of her robe in water, or receives

the god by inhaling vapours arising from it – in all these ways she becomes ready to partake of the external god.

Yet none of this arises as a result of any corporeal or animal power, nor by virtue of the surroundings or prophetic apparatus, but from the external presence of the god and from the fact that the priestess herself, before prophesying, has performed a multitude of ritual sacrifices, observed the sacred laws, bathed, fasted for three whole days and retired into the shrine, there to be blissfully irradiated at some length with the divine radiance. It is in such ways that the god is seen to be entreated by prayer to draw near, and that he becomes externally present, and not only is the prophetess, before she takes up her traditional place, inspired in the most wonderful way, but similarly, in the spirit that arises from the fountain, another, more ancient god, quite separate from the place, is seen to emerge – One who is the Original Cause of place, fountain and divining-technique alike.'

Thus, at least, Iamblichus.

Given that Nostradamus starts his whole prophetic work by citing these texts, there can be no doubt at all that verses I.1 and I.2 describe his own basic divinatory practices, too. The seer had first to get himself into the right meditative frame of mind (he refers on several occasions to the need to calm the mind beforehand). He had to bathe, fast and possibly abstain from sex for at least three days, as well as cutting himself off both from his family and from visitors. We know, indeed, that he tended to conduct his seances at dead of night between midnight and four in the morning, which would of course have had much the same effect. Then, seating himself on some kind of metal tripod above a pool or bowl of water giving off aromatic vapours – and in which he had previously dipped his feet and the hem of his ritual gown — he would immerse himself in prayer and await the god's arrival.

Sitting there amid the fumes and the nocturnal stillness, his mind imbued with the specialness and sanctity of the occasion, it is not too surprising that he soon started to see lights, rather like sparks or small flames, in the darkness, and perhaps dreamlike visions too. The typical effects of sensory deprivation are well known, especially when aromatic fumes are added to the equation. From time to time, too, odd words would seemingly pop into his mind, and possibly he could just about manage to maintain the trance while scribbling them down on a pad by his side.

True, we have only his word for it. But his description of the preparatory calming of his mind seems suspiciously genuine, as does his description of the after-effects. His visions, he says in his letter to the King, came to him 'comme dans un mirouer ardant'. True, numerous commentators with more credulity than sense have seen in this phrase a description of some kind of magic mirror surrounded by flames in which he could somehow see the future. The supposed device has even figured in paintings of him. In fact, though, 'un mirouer ardant' (the term is also used by Rabelais) is simply a burning-mirror — a concave mirror not unlike a shaving mirror, with which the sun's rays could be concentrated on a single spot.

Try looking into such a mirror when next you get the chance, and you will see precisely what he meant.

Q. If he didn't actually have a magic mirror after all, how about the idea that he is supposed to have done it all by 'scrying' — concentrating his eyes on a candle flame or a bowl of water?

A. He may conceivably have done this. I myself have reported the idea. But the only sources on which commentators who suggest it normally base the assertion are the two verses on p. 97 and the associated comments in the accompanying letters. The original texts on which they are based suggest nothing of the kind.

Theurgy

The 'fearful voice' mentioned by the seer, however, is a bit of a conundrum. Nowhere is such a phenomenon mentioned by Iamblichus. This could suggest that Nostradamus didn't merely make the appropriate personal preparations and immerse himself in prayer, but engaged in active dialogue with the god to the extent of actually commanding him or it to reveal the future.

This, if so, is highly redolent of ritual magic – the kind of ritual magic for summoning up spirits and commanding their obedience that is to be found in the great magical *grimoires* such as the ancient *Clavicula Salomonis* or 'Key of Solomon'. Such things were, after all, all the rage at the time. In fact Nostradamus's near-contemporary, the English court astrologer Dr John Dee, would make a considerable living out of conjuring up spirits during the later years of the century.

The first book of the *Clavicula Salomonis* starts with tables of the planets, angels, archangels, metals and colours that are ritually appropriate to each hour of each day of the week (this certainly seems to chime with what Nostradamus describes in his letter to François Bérard: see p. 104). It then goes into the necessary personal preparations – continence, abstinence from vain conversation, ritual bathing, self-exorcism, the donning of clean, white robes, the choice of time, place and weather, the various ritual accoutrements, the flame, the fumigations, the magic circles and the prayers that must go with them. Then follows the great conjuration commanding the spirits to appear, which invokes the power of God Himself. Further conjurations of ever-increasing power are added, in case the spirits in question prove uncooperative. These incorporate ever more thunderous commands, along with a variety of correspondingly blood-curdling threats (to me, all rather reminiscent of the various hotnesses of Indian curry!). If the worst comes to the worst, a powerful ritual curse is added, but otherwise the ritual is given for dismissing the spirits again once they have done your bidding – which in this case, clearly, means revealing full details of the future event currently under consideration.

As the legendary Sorcerer's Apprentice found out to his cost, it is vital to know not merely the spell, but the counter-spell, too!

Next follows an important section on how to construct the necessary Hebrew-inscribed 'pentacles' or magic designs. The Second Pentacle of Saturn incorporates (interestingly enough, in the light of the seer's letter to François Bérard) the celebrated multidimensional acrostic:

```
S A T O R
A R E P O
T E N E T
O P E R A
R O T A S
```

which is based on the Latin words 'PATER NOSTER' ('Our Father'), plus the letters 'A' and 'O', equivalent to Alpha and Omega, the first and last letters of the Greek alphabet. Further sections explain how to recover stolen goods (one wonders whether Nostradamus himself secretly used this rite when divining what had happened to the treasures stolen from the canons of Orange in 1561), to say nothing of how to become invisible, how to stop sportsmen from killing game, how to make magic garters and a magic carpet, and so on.

Book two goes over some of the ground again. The correct hours and lunar positions for the various rites are prescribed, as is the personal conduct of the Master of the Art and his disciples. Fasting, diet, robes, shoes, prayers and the other preparatory rituals and accoutrements are once again described – including the knife, sword, sickle, poniard, dagger, lance, wand and staff. The methods of fumigation with incense, perfumes and other odours are laid down, together with the way of preparing the ritual water and odoriferous spices. After a section on the ritual fire, directions are offered for the preparation of the pen (in this case either a goose-quill or one from a swallow or crow) as well as of the paper or parchment, followed by instructions for the use of bat and other animal blood, wax, earth, iron instruments, silk cloth and the various magical characters. The book concludes with directions for performing the necessary ritual sacrifices.

Did Nostradamus, then, indulge in such practices?

The signs are that he probably did. However, he clearly had reservations about it. Such things, he seems to have felt, were a bit like psychic gunpowder, liable to blow up in the practitioner's face. Consequently, once he had done with them he burnt the relevant magic books and warned his son off such practices. So, at least, he claimed. 'Fantasies and vanities', he called them in his *Préface*, and warned that they 'desiccate the body and send the soul to perdition, while troubling the feeble sense'.

Which does, it has to be said, suggest a man who has actually tried them and knows what he is talking about.

That, then, appears to be the sum of Nostradamus's supplementary techniques, apart from ... :

Incubation

Curiously, this technique – which amounts to a kind of cross between 'sleeping on it' and dream therapy – is not mentioned in the *Propheties* or their accompanying letters. However, in his letter of 27 August 1562 to François Bérard, alchemist, lawyer and Procurator Fiscal to the Papal Legation at Avignon, Nostradamus goes into considerable detail about it. In an attempt to assess the qualities of the latter's magic ring, he says, he has spent nine nights in succession from midnight until four in the morning, his head crowned with laurel and wearing the said ring with its blue stone on his finger, and using the Delphic technique to quiz its indwelling spirit. The result was an oracle in Latin verse that purported (once he had changed the prescribed goose-quill for a more promising swan-feather) to be in some kind of automatic writing – i.e. writing produced while in a state of trance.

After posing additional questions to the spirit about various alchemical techniques, he then put the laurels beneath his pillow, placed a further crown of laurel on his head and girded himself with a garland of periwinkles. He next prayed to his guardian angel with the words: 'Angel who art my guardian and governest me, let me prophesy on the transformation of the things of nature, as from atop a brazen tripod, according to the movements of the stars. Hear me, I beseech thee, by the friendly silences of the moon, by these shadows which Mars casts suddenly at his rising. Hear me, I say, with the aid of the most good and omnipotent Christ and of the Holy Virgin Mother, and of Michael the Archangel my invincible patron ...'

And so on and so on, through a whole series of requests for guidance in matters alchemical, to which the angel, appearing in a dream, replied via a further verse-oracle in Latin.

Finally quizzing the angel regarding Bérard's future prospects, he received a third oracle, which he wrote down in turn.

Q. Is it true that Nostradamus used alchemy and the Kabbala in making his prophecies?

A. Certainly he was familiar with alchemy, but apart from the above and a series of ostensible alchemical references at verses IV.28 to IV.30 he makes no specific reference to using it for prophetic purposes. As for the Kabbala, it is clear that it could at least have played a role in his theurgical practices. However, in his letter of 20 January 1562 to two correspondents called Dominique de Saint-Étienne and Jammot Pathon he is pretty dismissive about people who attempt to use it directly for prophetic purposes. This suggests, then, that he himself didn't use it in this way.

As for the apparent pieces of 'automatic writing', all of them turned out to be carefully composed pieces of Latin verse incorporating acrostics on Nostradamus's own name and that of Bérard. They were exceedingly obtuse, admittedly, but there was little evidence of any specific trance state as such, let alone the gobbledygook that automatic writing can so easily produce.

What seems to have happened, in fact, was that the seer had taken his inspiration at least in part from the letters of the two names. He had, in a sense, been inspired by language itself.

This leads us to the inevitable conclusion that his final technique was simply ...

Linguistic Inspiration

This technique would not be too surprising, given that language was the corner-stone on which virtually the whole vast enterprise of the Renaissance was based. It was language that was supposed to reveal all the secrets of the past in the form of books and manuscripts. And so now, in Nostradamus's case, it was language that must reveal the mysteries of the future too.

No wonder, then, that he would couch his prophecies in verse. For now the very word with which the presumably 'inspired' first line of each successive verse ended would control the corresponding rhyming-word at the end of line 3, and thus to some extent line 3 itself. This in turn would control the way in which line 2 led from line 1 to line 3, while the need to rhyme the last word of line 2 with that of line 4 would go on to determine the content of line 4.

And the whole of it would of course be further 'inspired' by the need to get precisely ten syllables into each line, to say nothing of the 'caesura', or pause, that was conventionally required after the fourth syllable of each line.

Language, certainly, had a logic and magic of its own. What better medium than verse, then, for his guiding divinity to express itself through?

9

Be Your Own
Nostradamus

As he himself pointed out, there was nothing superhuman about Michel Nostradamus. Consequently, given that his techniques are more or less known, there is absolutely no reason why you should not apply at least the more straightforward of them for yourself.

Before you do so, however, there are two main things to bear in mind. The first is that the seer's whole approach was based on the idea that 'there's nothing new under the sun'. The result was a series of predictions based on the idea that earlier events would at length repeat themselves, in time with the revolutions of the planets. You should not expect, therefore, to use his techniques to predict events that have never occurred before.

Q. But what about those verses – IX.83, X.74, II.13 and III.2, for example – that seem to predict events leading up to the end of the world? Surely they have never happened before?

A. If what we have established thus far is valid, the answer has to be either that these particular prophecies are not really about end-of-the-world events after all, or that something very like them has indeed happened before. Alternatively, they may represent an attempt by Nostradamus to add authority to his predictions simply by including events already prophesied by St John's Revelation, albeit without necessarily dating them. On the whole, this last seems the most likely.

The second thing to bear in mind is that Nostradamus amplified the resulting predictions with divinatory techniques drawn mainly from the essentially Apollonian practices of ancient Delphi and Branchidai – techniques that are not necessarily as easy for us to reproduce or control today. You should therefore not count on being able to follow him too far into this area.

Clearly, then, the first and main thing is to concentrate on the astrological side of things. Only then, if you are so inclined, should you think of trying to apply his more arcane techniques.

1. *Select the past event whose repetition you wish to predict*

There is no particular method in this: you need merely take the first event that comes into your mind. Nostradamus would probably have regarded this as opening yourself up to the Divine will. You, however, are at liberty to regard it in any light you like.

By way of example, let us take the dramatic death of Diana, Princess of Wales in a car crash in 1997.

2. *Note carefully all the details of that event*

This means establishing precisely where, when and under what circumstances it occurred, and especially the exact latitude. In the case of Princess Diana, the date was 31 August 1997 (for this particular astrological technique no exact time is necessary, though it is worth noting that it was early in the morning), and the place was the centre of Paris. This gives the latitude as 48°52′ North. As for the other circumstances, the princess was killed with her lover in a black car being driven at high speed by a drunk driver through an underpass close to the river Seine. The bodyguard who was also present survived the crash. Any or all of these circumstances (plus any yet to be revealed) may well be repeated in the course of the future event, too, and so should be noted.

3. *Using a suitable ephemeris, establish the positions of all the planets during at least the previous month*

If you have either a printed or a computerised planetary ephemeris, look up – and if necessary print out – the tables for July and August 1997. If you are using a computer, though, be sure to establish the correct parameters first. Recommended are:

> Midnight positions
> Tropical zodiac
> Greenwich Mean Time
> True positions
> Gregorian calendar

In the case of an original event before September 1752 in England, or before October 1582 in the countries of the former Catholic Europe, you should of course substitute the Julian calendar for the Gregorian one (see p. 114).

4. *Again using a suitable ephemeris, find the next occasion on which at least five, and preferably six, of the same planets are in exactly the same signs as in 3 above.*

To my knowledge, there is, at the time of writing, no computer program to do this. You will therefore need to do a manual search, concentrating on the same time of year (which will tend to ensure that the sun at least is one of the bodies in question!). This can be quite demanding, but it can help to know that certain known periodicities apply. For example, for any given time of year there is a tendency for the planets out as far as Saturn to regroup in their former signs every 236 years or so – or, more comprehensively, every 944 years or so. Within that pattern, however, certain 'sub-loops' also occur. In particular there is a notable 59-year sub-loop, tied to the revolutions of Jupiter and Saturn, that typically runs for only two cycles at a time – thus offering three potential 'matches' in the course of that period.

In the case of Princess Diana's death, for example, such a 59-year sub-loop does indeed apply, giving a six-planet match (including the moon) between July/August 1997 on the one hand and August 2056 on the other. (You can verify this from your own tables (see p.114).)

Where such a search results in a near-miss, it is worth remembering that Saturn tends to stay in each sign for about two and a half years at a time, Jupiter for about a year and Mars for about two months, depending on whether they have spent any time going retrograde (i.e. backwards) in the interim. Subject to these parameters, it may sometimes pay to search the year before or after your 'match' if your initial search proves unsuccessful.

Meanwhile, be sure that you are still observing the same parameters as before, with the exception that you should in any case now be using the Gregorian calendar.

5. *Fix the precise beginnings and ends of the 'match' on the two charts in question*

Eventually, then, you should discover a period – perhaps just a day or two, or possibly as much as several weeks – when the sun plus four or five of the planets are in exactly the same signs as they were originally. By seeking, within that period, the points at which there is also a *lunar* match, you can now narrow the period down to its finest possible extent.

Theoretically at least, you now have the exact future period during which there is the potential for a similar royal personage to meet a similar fate under similar circumstances.

In the case of Diana, the details of the match are shown on the two horographs below, which depict all the relevant planetary positions at the times of the original and future events – as well as the irrelevant ones. You will note that the match in question is actually between 28 July and 16 August 1997 on the one hand, and 3 and 22 August 2056 on the other – which beg to be seen as the two *periods of causation*.

6. *In order to establish the latitude of the future event, find or calculate the noon solar declination for the beginning and end of the original period (to the nearest degree)*

True, not all planetary ephemerides give solar declinations (i.e. the height of the sun, relative to the celestial equator, on any given day of the year). Neither the popular *American Ephemeris* nor most computerised

HOROGRAPH FOR: 28th July 1997   **TO:** 16th August 1997

	Aries	Tauru	Gemin	Cance	Leo	Virgo	Libra	Scorp	Sagit	Capri	Aquar	Pisce
Pluto									✷			
Neptune										✷		
Uranus											✷	
Saturn	★											
Jupiter											★	
Mars							✷					
Venus						★						
Mercury						★						
Moon		★	★	★	★	★	★	★	★	★		
Sun					★							

Solar noon declination (to nearest degree): 19°N to 14°N

Geographical latitude: 48°52' N

LOCATION: Paris, France
EVENT: Death of Diana Princess of Wales

HOROGRAPH FOR:	3rd August 2056					TO:	22nd August 2056				
	Aries	Tauru	Gemin	Cance	Leo	Virgo	Libra	Scorp	Sagit	Capri	Aquar	Pisce
Pluto												☆
Neptune			☆									
Uranus							☆					
Saturn	★											
Jupiter											★	
Mars			☆									
Venus						★						
Mercury						★						
Moon		★	★	★	★	★	★	★	★	★		
Sun					★							

Solar noon declination (to nearest degree): 17°N to 12°N

Relative latitude: 2°S   Geographical latitude: 46°52' N (±1°)

POSSIBLE LOCATION: Bern, Switzerland
EVENT: Death of future 'goddess of the moon'

113

ephemerides that I have seen volunteer this information. The *Concise Planetary Ephemeris* published by the Hieratic Publishing Co., however, does volunteer the necessary data, albeit only for every third day (which will of course involve some sensible interpolation on your part). So do various almanacs and sets of astronomical tables, such as those provided by *Reed's Nautical Almanac* – though this last deals with only one year at a time.

By hook or by crook, then, you are going to have to acquire such tables or to borrow or copy a set. Be sure to copy the figures for at least four consecutive years, so that you can base your calculations on a comparable year relative to the nearest leap year (i.e. one – not counting those century-years indivisible by 400 – whose last two figures are divisible by 4).

If your 'original event' is early enough to fall under the Julian calendar, you will need to ask your computer to convert the relevant dates to Gregorian ones before establishing the solar declination on the above basis. After doing so you can pinpoint the corresponding dates by taking the day when the sun is in exactly the same number of degrees of the same sign (the difference between the two calendars ranges from virtually nothing at the time of Christ, via ten days at the time of Nostradamus, to 13 days now).

In the present case you will need to find or calculate the noon solar declinations on 28 July and 16 August 1997 respectively. These work out at 19° North and 14° North respectively, as entered on the first horograph above.

Be sure to distinguish carefully between declination North (i.e. above the celestial equator) and declination South (i.e. below the celestial equator).

7. *Now calculate the noon solar declination for the beginning and end of the future period, once again to the nearest degree*

This is carried out in exactly the same way as in 6 above. This time the figures for the death of the *future* 'Princess Diana' work out at 17° North and 12° North respectively, as per the second horograph above.

8. *Calculate, on the basis of 6 and 7 above, the relative noon solar declination between the two events*

In other words, subtract the solar declination for the start of the original period from that for the start of the future event: this will give either a plus or a minus quantity. Then do the same for the ends of the two periods. Note the two figures.

In the present case they both work out at −2° (or 2° South), as per the second horograph.

9. *Now apply the 'corrections' that you have just calculated to the latitude of the original event*

The latitude of central Paris is 48°52′ North. Subtracting two degrees from this gives the future latitude as 46°52′ North, plus or minus one degree.

10. *Find the location (on the latitude that you have just established) whose characteristics best match those of the original location*

In the present case it needs to be a capital city − probably, like Paris, in Europe − that stands on a river crossed by numerous bridges, and that has at very least a cathedral and an important university. If it also has a notable tower and a large triumphal arch, so much the better.

In the event, the best and most obvious match is Bern (or Berne), the capital of Switzerland, which stands at latitude

46°57' North — or within only five miles or so of the ideal figure.

11. *Now write down the first line of verse that comes into your head to describe the event in general terms*

If you wish to write in the English equivalent of Nostradamus's style, you will need to cast it in the form of an iambic pentameter — i.e. a line whose rhythm goes 'de-dum de-dum de-dum de-dum de-dum' or, inverting one or more of the five 'feet', 'dum-de de-dum de-dum de-dum de-dum' ... or whatever.

This is your first piece of 'inspiration'. Treasure it, for it has to serve as the basis for what must now follow.

In my own case the first line came out as: '*In Bern, alas, shall chaste Diana die*', which may seem dangerously explicit about the name of the Princess's future counterpart until you realise that 'chaste Diana' is a traditional expression not for a human being, but for *the goddess of the moon*, while the word 'chaste' is a homonym of the highly significant word 'chased'.

12. *Apply whatever further techniques now most appeal to you for engaging your unconscious in the prophetic process*

To take them in turn:

Divination If the gentle rites of Apollo as practised at Delphi and Branchidai appeal to you, find out all you can about them. Next, acquire any of the associated paraphernalia that you deem to be necessary and helpful — tripod, wand, white robe, laurels, aromatic substances, goose-and/or swan-quill and so on — and assemble them in some quiet, secluded place for your long nocturnal ritual. Finally, after preparing yourself through abstinence, quietness and ritual bathing, meditate on any or all of Apollo's typical symbols – pre-eminently the sun ('the sun at night', as Nostradamus put it), then the lyre, the bow and arrow, the stag, mouse, ass, goat, ram, wolf, tortoise, dolphin, serpent, quail, crow, kite, white raven, vulture, swan, goose, apple, palm tree, olive and laurel. Then, when the hour comes around, use whatever meditative techniques you are familiar with to forget all the cares of the world and sink into a state of pure contemplation on the event in question and the single line of verse that you have written – and invoke Apollo himself to appear and grant you the gift of prophecy. Beware, though – you are unlikely to be fit for anything much the next day!

Theurgy Here you would be treading on much more dramatic and dangerous ground. If you insist on venturing into this territory, you will need to acquire a copy of the *Clavicula Salomonis* or 'Key of Solomon' (see Further Reading) and follow it to the letter. However, in the light of Nostradamus's own warnings in the preface to his son, and the awful example of figures such as the infamous Aleister Crowley, you would be well advised to avoid this technique completely – not least because, should anyone hear you, you are likely to find yourself carted off to the nearest padded cell . . .

Incubation Of all the techniques available, this is most to be recommended for modern people living in the modern world. Whether or not you care to follow the exact ritual practised by Nostradamus (see Chapter 8), the main point is that you should hold both the event and your single line of verse in your mind as you fall asleep at night. As a result, it is quite likely that, when you wake up in the morning, you will find all kinds of ideas floating around in your head, and possibly even suitable phrases for writing them down in. Alternatively, you may actually dream the outcome. Either way, note down the results quickly before you forget them. For this reason, you should keep a pad and pencil by your bedside. After all, your inspiration may come suddenly and unexpectedly, like a thief in the night.

13. *Finally, use the insights that have surfaced in the meantime to compose your complete verse-prophecy*

Typically, Nostradamus seems to have written not one, but two verses for each event. Whether or not you choose to follow this precedent, do avoid making either the future date or the details of your prediction too rigid or definite. Fate has a wonderful gift for fulfilling predictions in the most original and unexpected of ways!

In my own case, for example, the two verses finally came out as follows:

> *In Bern, alas, shall chaste Diana die,*
> *In love with love and speeding in her car,*
> *Before the sun Venus and Mercury*
> *In Virgo joins, or Jupiter her star.*

> *Mighty the shock that such a great princess,*
> *So young, so vital, should depart so soon:*
> *A sea of flowers shall mark a world's distress*
> *When night reclaims the lady of the moon.*

10

Where Can I Find Out More?

European/North American publishers are indicated by slash marks.

Books

See Further Reading on p. 124. Most French titles are available from the Maison de Nostradamus, rue Nostradamus, 13300 Salon-de-Provence, France (ask for an order form).

Original Texts

The exquisite original 1555 (Bonhomme) edition (verses I.1 to IV.53, plus the Preface to César) was rediscovered and republished in facsimile by Michel Chomarat in 1984, but is now out of print. Your best plan is to bribe somebody who has it to photocopy it for you. It is reprinted in transliterated form in my *Nostradamus Encyclopedia* (see Further Reading).

The rather more scruffy but none the less informative

1557 (Du Rosne) edition (verses I.1 to VII.40, plus the Preface to César) is available in facsimile from Editions Michel Chomarat, 160 rue Vendôme, F-69003, Lyon, France, or from the Maison de Nostradamus (address on p.119; ask for an order form). Verses IV.54 to VII.40 from this edition are printed in transliterated form in my *Nostradamus Encyclopedia*.

The complete 1568 (Benoist Rigaud) edition of the *Centuries* is transcribed fairly reliably in John Hogue's massive *Nostradamus: The Complete Prophecies* (Element/Element 1997) and (minus the Preface to César and the Letter to Henri II) Erika Cheetham's *The Final Prophecies of Nostradamus* (Futura, 1989/Perigree, 1989), though 'reliable' is unfortunately the last word that should be applied to their accompanying translations and interpretations. The texts of verses VII.42 to X.100 are also reprinted in my *Nostradamus Encyclopedia*.

Many of the *Présages* and *Sixains* (1605) are to be found in Jean-Charles de Fontbrune's *Nostradamus 1* and *Nostradamus 2* (Pan, 1984 or Henry Holt/Owl, NY, 1987), albeit with 'translations' that are more in the nature of highly skewed interpretations. The original texts (somewhat edited) of all the *Propheties* – and much more – in a variety of editions are also included in Edgar Leoni's *Nostradamus and His Prophecies* and (in the 1568 and 1605 editions) in John Hogue's *Nostradamus: The Complete Prophecies*, as well as (in the original editions) in my *Nostradamus Encyclopedia*.

A version of part two of Nostradamus's cookbook, the *Traité des fardemens et des confitures*, can be obtained from the Maison de Nostradamus (address above) under the title *Traité des confitures*. However, the original book's purported English translation, *The Elixirs of Nostradamus* (Bloomsbury, 1995), is not recommended if you are planning to apply it, as many of the items in this translation of a revision of a translation are (not surprisingly) mistranslated, and could possibly poison you. Also available from the Maison de Nostradamus are his *Orus Apollo* (a curious and highly flawed work in verse on Egyptian hieroglyphs) and various other publications including a facsimile of his 1565 letter to Queen Catherine de Médicis as printed and published in the year of his death, 1566. Once again, send for an order form.

Videos and Films

The Maison de Nostradamus can supply a reasonably reliable video in French (*Nostradamus: Prophète de l'an 2000?*), but this is fairly limited in scope. Virtually all the rest (to say nothing of the film *Nostradamus*) are ludicrously inaccurate – though *The Man Who Saw Tomorrow* (Warner Home Videos), narrated by Orson Welles, is at least well produced, if heavily Cheetham-based.

Internet Websites

There is a huge number of alleged Nostradamus Websites on the Internet. Many of them, though, have little or nothing to do with the real Nostradamus or what his prophecies actually say. Even the following list of some of the more useful of them offers no guarantee of up-to-dateness or necessary relevance.

http://www.angelfire.com/biz/Nosty/index.html
http://www.globalxs.nl/home/n/nijweide/prophecy
/nostradamus.html
http://prophetic.simplenet.com/elysium/
http://www.telebyte.nl/~zaphod/nostra.html
http://prophetic.simplenet.com/cwn1.htm
http://prophetic.simplenet.com/websites.htm

http://www.infobahnos.com/~ledash/
quebec_prophecy.html
http://www.alumni.caltech.edu/~jamesf/nostradam
us.html
http://www.alumni.caltech.edu/~jamesf/Nfaqs.html
http://myweb.worldnet.fr/~dhuicq/soleils/
lien0053.htm
http://myweb.worldnet.fr/~dhuicq/soleils/
trah0054.htm
http://www.infobahnos.com/~ledash/nostra.html
http://www.infobahnos.com/~ledash/
nostradamus.html
http://www.nostradamususa.com/
http://www.mindspring.com/~psciqliano/prophecy
http://www.m–m.org/jz/spiritee.html

Internet Newsgroups

A lively Nostradamus Newsgroup is to be found at:

alt.prophecies.nostradamus

and would welcome both your enquiries and your input. Be
warned, however. Like all such newsgroups, it is full of
nutters, paranoids, megalomaniacs and would-be Messiahs *as
well as* serious enquirers and Nostradamus scholars.

For Further Details and Latest Information

Contact or visit the Maison de Nostradamus (address on
p.119, open all year during normal hours, with some excep-
tions at weekends), which can supply a whole range not only

of the French editions listed above, but also a number of facsimiles, plus a series of magazines entitled the *Cahiers Nostradamus* and containing more facsimiles, extracts from the *Almanachs* and so on.

Further Reading

European/North American publishers are indicated by slash marks.

Amadou, R.: *L'Astrologie de Nostradamus* (ARRC, Poissy, 1992/).
Limited edition dossier including a variety of texts and horoscopes, including French versions of all 51 of the letters to and from Nostradamus printed by Dupèbe (see below).
Benazra, R.: *Répertoire Chronologique Nostradamique (1545–1989)* (Trédaniel, 1990/).
Bibliographical survey (in French) of all Nostradamus's writings and editions (up to the time of writing).
Brind'Amour, P.: *Nostradamus astrophile* (/University of Ottawa, 1993).
A superb and comprehensive examination in French of all matters relating to Nostradamus's astrology, albeit by a respected academic who didn't believe in the seer's prophetic powers.
Brind'Amour, P.: *Nostradamus: Les premières centuries ou propheties* (Droz, 1996/).

A wonderfully clear and thorough French exposition of the first 353 of Nostradamus's prophecies, quoted in both versions of the original 1555 edition.

Chomarat, M., Dupèbe, J. and Polizzi, G.: *Nostradamus ou le savoir transmis* (Chomarat, 1997/).

A French academic symposium, mainly on the links between ancient events and Nostradamus's predictions.

Chomarat, M. and Laroche, Dr. J.-P.: *Bibliographie Nostradamus* (Koerner, 1989/).

The best French source for all details of early editions up to 1800.

Dupèbe, J.: *Nostradamus. Lettres Inédites* (Droz, 1983/).

Fifty-one hitherto unpublished private letters to and from Nostradamus, mainly in Latin.

Iamblichus of Chalcis: (ed. Roman, S.) *On the Mysteries: De mysteriis Aegyptiorum* (Chthonios Books, 1989/).

Two English translations (by Taylor and Wilder – printed side by side) of this seminal Greek work on which Nostradamus based much of his methodology.

Laver, J.: *Nostradamus or the Future Foretold* (Mann, 1942–81/).

A respected, though now dated, introductory survey.

Lemesurier, P.: *The Nostradamus Encyclopedia* (Godsfield/St Martin's, 1997).

By far the most informative and comprehensive English-language reference book to date, including all the prophecies in their earliest editions with paraphrases, plus a Nostradamus dictionary and concordance.

Leoni, E: *Nostradamus and his Prophecies* (/Wings, 1961–82).

A wonderfully comprehensive, if now somewhat dated survey of the subject, incorporating all the prophecies (though not in very reliable versions) with very literal English translations.

Leroy, Dr. E.: *Nostradamus: ses origines, sa vie, son oeuvre* (Lafitte, 1993/).

The original French source-book, based on carefully researched archives, for everything to do with Nostradamus, his life, family, work and origins, though already becoming rather dated.

Mathers, S. Liddell MacGregor (ed. and tr.): *The Key of Solomon the King* (Routledge and Kegan Paul, 1972/).

The famous 1888 English translation.

Nostradamus, M.: *Orus Apollo* (ed. Rollet, P., as *Interprétation des hiéroglyphes de Horapollo*) (Marcel Petit, 1993/).

Nostradamus's verse translation of an extremely dubious work on Egyptian hieroglyphs, incorporating a facsimile of a page of what appears to be original manuscript.

Nostradamus, M.: *Les Propheties, Lyon, 1557* (Chomarat, 1993/).

Facsimile of the 1557 edition.

Nostradamus, M.: *Lettre à Catherine de Médicis* (Chomarat, 1996/).

Another of Michel Chomarat's beautifully produced facsimiles.

Nostradamus, M.: *Traité des fardemens et des confitures*, published as *Le Vray et Parfaict Embellissement de la Face* in Plantin's Antwerp edition of 1557 (Gutenberg Reprints, 1979/).

Facsimile of Nostradamus's best-selling treatise on preparing cosmetics and conserves.

Ward, C.A.: *Oracles of Nostradamus* (Society of Metaphysicians (facsimile of 1891 edn), 1990, 1995/Modern Library (Scribner), 1940).

An early survey of Nostradamus and his prophecies, interesting mainly as a historical document in its own right.

Index

Piatkus Guides, written by experts, combine background information with practical exercises, and are designed to change the way you live. Titles include:

Tarot Cassandra Eason

Tarot's carefully graded advice enables readers to obtain excellent readings from Day One. You will quickly gain a thorough knowledge of both Major and Minor Arcanas and their symbolism, and learn how to use a variety of Tarot spreads.

Meditation Bill Anderton

Meditation covers the origins, theory and benefits of meditation. It includes over 30 meditations and provides all the advice you need to meditate successfully.

Crystal Wisdom Andy Baggott and Sally Morningstar

Crystal Wisdom is a fascinating guide to the healing power of crystals. It details the history and most popular modern uses of crystals and vibrational healing. It also covers colour, sound and chakra healing, and gem, crystal and flower essences.

Celtic Wisdom Andy Baggott

Celtic Wisdom is a dynamic introduction to this popular subject. The author covers Celtic spirituality, the wisdom of trees, animals and stones, ritual and ceremony and much more.

Feng Shui Jon Sandifer

Feng Shui introduces the origins, theory and practice of the Chinese art of perfect placement, or geomancy. It provides easy-to-follow techniques to help you carry out your own readings and create an auspicious living space.

The Essential Nostradamus Peter Lemesurier

The Essential Nostradamus charts the life of this extraordinary man, and includes newly discovered facts about his life and work. Peter Lemesurier unravels his prophecies for the coming decades.